the Work of Children

*For dear Isabel,
With affection
and best wishes as
you persevere in your
good work !*

*Esther
30 April 2011*

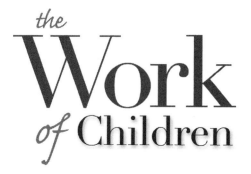

the Work *of* Children

HELPING CHILDREN UNDERSTAND THE MEANING, PURPOSE, AND VALUE OF WORK

Esther Joos Esteban, Ph.D.

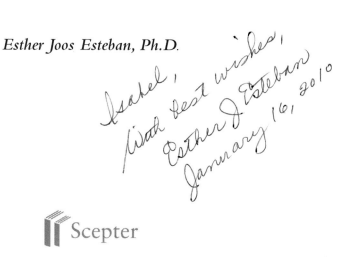

Scepter

*Dedicated to Papa and Mama for
their inspiration and example of
good work*

Copyright © 2009, Scepter Publishers, Inc.
P.O. Box 211, New York, N.Y. 10018
www.scepterpublishers.org

ISBN: 13-978-1-59417-082-9

PRINTED IN THE UNITED STATES OF AMERICA

Contents

Acknowledgments

Some trips are taken alone while others are best made with many. The writing of this book is clearly an example of the latter. Without the collective experiences, insights, and suggestions of family, friends, colleagues, experts, and even strangers, this manuscript might still be a journey waiting to happen.

I extend my deepest gratitude to the following persons who guided me along the way:

- For reading the manuscript and adding invaluable commentaries derived from their personal and professional experience: my sister, Loretta Saunderson, Sara Brescher, Socorro Claudio, Rhoda Lubetkin, and sons, Enrique and Anton.

- For their expertise in child development based on years of observation and daily work with children: Grace Bautista, Kathy Mehr, Barbara Nicholls, Carla Villacorta, and niece Pamela Voelksen.

- For her meaningful recommendations on the work of children as environmentalists: Angelina Galang.

- For the professional expertise of Scepter Publishers, Inc: publisher, John Powers, editor, Russell Shaw, and proof reader, Arlene Borg.

- For their continuing encouragement throughout the process: husband, Enrique, daughters Christine and Cindy, sons-in-law, Ajay Munshi and Andreas Coppi, and grandchildren Nikhil,

Maya, and Carlo; Department of Education at the University of Asia and the Pacific, Manila, Philippines; and Department of Psychology at Miriam College, Manila, Philippines.

- For their suggestions, support, and friendship: Cynthia Ballat, Jim Damaso, Nanette Diyco, Gladys Golo, Soledad Navarro, Lourdes Romero, Carol Tan, Rita Tuason, and Tootsie Vicente.

- For his inspiration and teachings on the value and nobility of ordinary duties in work: St. Josemaria Escriva.

Thank you! You helped *The Work of Children* reach its destination.

Introduction

Papa had a black metal lunchbox. It was sturdy and austere, time-worn after many years of use. Mama filled it each day with a thermos of coffee and generous portions of her hearty German cooking. At 6 p.m., Papa brought it home again, empty after a day of work. Mama cleaned it and then it sat on the pantry shelf, waiting to be filled the next morning. Here was a predictable cycle of recurring images. Mama, Papa, the lunchbox, and work. As a child I always associated them. They formed a team . . . simple and dependable.

This enduring and reassuring scene also played out in the homes of our relatives and friends, most of whom had migrated with my parents from the southwestern province of Germany, Baden Wurttemberg, during the 1920s and 1930s. Like Mama and Papa, many were highly skilled craftsmen and technicians, some were farmers or laborers, still others were businessmen, academicians, and scientists. They brought with them a rich cultural heritage of work ethics that they applied with fervor and determination in their adopted homeland.

In time, they passed on a legacy of good work to their children. With remarkable naturalness, they conveyed the importance and dignity of work. With simplicity, they taught that hard work develops minds and bodies. While working together, they inspired teamwork that builds families, communities, and a nation. With steadfastness, they role-modeled self-discipline and perseverance worthy of imitation.

The simple, sturdy black metal lunchbox is an image for entire generations of workers who labored to build industrialized America. As immigrant parents, Mama and Papa were intent upon creating a better life for us children. *Giving example of good work* and *training in work*—these were the primary tools they used to foster understanding, attitudes, skills, and virtues at work. Their strategies are as relevant and universal today as they were then. Today, the third generation in our family continues to reap the benefits.

Twenty years in the making, *The Work of Children* started out as a book to keep the spirit of Mama and Papa alive among their grandchildren. But the unfinished manuscript lay dormant until recently, when their great-grandson (my grandson), when asked what he was doing, at age two exclaimed, "Grandma, I'm busy doing my work." His remarkable response motivated the retrieval of the faded pages, handwritten long before I had learned the wonders of Microsoft Word.

The Work of Children seeks to highlight the universal phenomenon of work, inspire parents to probe into its essence, and guide them as they help their children internalize the what, why, and how of work. It intends to revitalize an appreciation of work, often taken for granted, overlooked, and undervalued; it hopes to motivate renewed role modeling and good parenting practices.

The book is not about child labor, although the issue of child exploitation is of extraordinary concern and deserving of worldwide research and intervention. It is also not a step-by-step guide, even though suggestions and practical tips have been included. Nor does the book guarantee that, once read, parents will then automatically form their children into a highly inspired and efficient workforce. Only a young person who acknowledges the function and value of work and transcends purely material gratification can accomplish that for himself or herself.

Although much is said here about helping children acquire habits—virtues, that is—appropriate to the jobs and occupations of later life, it is important to understand that these good habits are also important for doing good work of any sort—not only paid employment outside the home but also the work done by housewives and mothers (and today, increasingly, by husbands and fathers) in the setting of home and family life, as well as unpaid volunteer work of all kinds. In short, this is a book about preparing children to do work of any variety, in any place, with commitment, competence, and a fulfilling sense of doing something useful and important.

Vignettes introduce the first four chapter themes. Each recalls a personal experience and some childhood impressions. The anecdotes are not meant to be idealized trips down memory lane. They simply highlight the chapter themes: the meaning, purpose, and value of work, and media's impact. The stories are promptly fast-forwarded to present realities of parents. Because of the integrative nature of the chapter themes, concepts necessarily recur or overlap.

In chapter 1, the caregiver reflects on the child's progressive understanding of the meaning of work in play, study, chores, hobbies, and activities; these are the forerunners of adult work. Chapter 2 presents the multiple dimensions and purposes of work and cautions parents about the impact that consumerism has on work attitudes. Chapter 3 further highlights the ethical dimension of work and emphasizes the dignity and virtues of the worker. In the fourth chapter, a sampling of research data suggests the strengths and limitations of multimedia exposure, the potential effects on the child's developing attitudes and habits towards work, and caregiver media management. A postscript examines the diagnosis of work as a *good* disease that everyone should be eager to catch!

Integrated in the first three chapters are *Opportune Moments*, which suggest specific strategies to elicit the child's participation and cooperation in work. They are organized according to the developmental stages of Early Childhood (0–6 years), Middle Childhood (7–12), and Adolescence (13–19). *Opportune Moments* are based on the developmental capabilities and needs of the child at each stage. Reasonable and appropriate activities are recommended that may be viewed as preventive measures and/or possibilities for intervention. (Caregivers, however, need to discern an individual child's abilities and readiness to undertake a suggested activity. They are challenged to be sensitive to the process of training, which is ongoing, flexible, and dependent on a host of variables, e.g., personal circumstances, environmental or cultural influences.) In chapter 4, the reader will find research studies that apply to each stage of development. They highlight special issues of exposure to media, e.g., violence and sexual content. Parenting strategies to help the child who is overexposed to media get back on track are discussed.

At the end of every chapter, *For Reflection* poses several questions for the caregiver's consideration, review, and resolution.

Depending on the reader's interests and objectives, *The Work of Children* can serve several purposes. The book is a *guide* to the function and dignity of work; a parenting or caregiver *manual*; and a *reference* for child development, family psychology and education, or human resource training, e.g., teacher training or parenting seminars. For readers who may wish to use it as a reference, *In Review*, at the end of the book, presents charts synthesizing essential concepts of each chapter.

Throughout the book, examples that concretize themes and application are drawn from personal encounters, interviews, focused group discussions, seminars, and e-mails with family, friends, colleagues, parents, teachers, students, and children who have willingly shared them with me. Except for family and friends, I have fictionalized names.

In an age of high technology, multimedia exposure, and consumerism, when our children and grandchildren may be distracted from the value, joy, and satisfaction of work, may this first volume help to restore and inspire insights and strategies that will transmit a legacy of good work. A second volume already in progress, *Children at Work: Fostering Good Work Habits*, highlights the development of diligence, order, cheerfulness, responsibility, and cooperation.

Esther Joos Esteban
New York City, 2009

Chapter 1

RECREATION:

The Meaning of Work

PAPA'S PERCEPTION OF WORK

"Papa must feel tired," I thought. After all, it was Saturday morning and last night I noticed the lines of fatigue etched on his face. "So why is he working again? Why doesn't he just rest and relax?"

Looking up at Papa, perched high on a ladder, I finally decided to ask.

"Papa," I called, straining my eyes against the bright morning sun. "Would you please answer a question for me?"

He was singing and painting the uppermost portions of our little white house, the modest two-story home that Mama and Papa were to occupy for forty years. He stopped singing . . . but never missing a stroke, replied, "*Ja*, sure. *Vat's* the *qwestion?*" in his thick German accent.

"Papa, why are you doing so much work again today? It's Saturday. Why don't you just rest?"

"Vork?" He looked puzzled, still managing the strokes rhythmically. With a smile and in a tone of warmth and naturalness, he responded, "Vy, dis isn't vork. *Dis is recreation!*" and he continued to sing and paint.

☒ ☒ ☒

That was my first verbal introduction to work. No lectures, no further explanations . . . simply a description to satisfy my eight-year-old curiosity.

I told my sister, Loretta, about my conversation with Papa. We both giggled at his answer and agreed that only our Papa would equate labor and toil with leisure and fun! It became a private joke between siblings.

In later years, as teenagers immersed in household chores of ironing and folding the laundry on Saturday morning, we would laugh and tease each other, "We know. This isn't work. This is recreation!" but we felt no resentment. How could we resist Papa's contagious, cheerful disposition toward work!

Probably without realizing it, Papa had cut to the core of work. Work or "recreation" is indeed a likely *re-creation* or realization of work, perhaps a continuation, or remake, or rediscovery, or an addition to work that has been undertaken before. Through every task that Papa accomplished, he intuitively grasped that he was participating in something bigger, in something that had started before, in something that was continuing, and in something that would be handed on. He felt privileged to work and perceived the dynamism and satisfaction of taking part in the process. As for his interpretation of work as recreation, i.e., diversion and leisure activity, I can only attribute this to his ability to find joy and great satisfaction in doing something that he perceived as worthwhile or creative and through which he gained mastery.

In his work as a family provider and tool and die maker, Papa understood basic functions of work:

Work enables the development of talents and capabilities.
Work requires focus and commitment.
Work inspires meaning and purpose in life.

Fast Forward

Almost five decades later, as I was checking up on the very quiet whereabouts of my two-year-old grandson, I called from the kitchen.

"Nikhil, where are you?"

"I'm here, Grandma," came a faint voice from the living room.

"What are you doing?" I asked.

Sitting there on the floor, immersed in a jigsaw puzzle, he answered, *"I'm busy doing my work, Grandma."* He was, in fact, totally engrossed in fitting the pieces of a puzzle together, developing eye-hand coordination and dexterity, and learning how to solve problems with attention and concentration.

Much like his great-grandfather, Nikhil had conceptualized his own version of the functions of work.

Work is an activity you do.
Work is a process that keeps you busy.
Work is a task that is your own.

At dinner that night, as I recounted the simple dialogue with Nikhil to my daughter, Christine, and son-in-law, Ajay, we found it easy to piece together how Nikhil had developed his ideas about work.

Unwittingly, all of us had used expressions or made comments about work.

Mommy: "Nikhil, I'm going to work at the office now, but I'll be home this afternoon."

Daddy: "I'll work from home today, Nikhil. I can play with you only after I have finished."

Grandma: "Nikhil, I'm busy working now. I'm baking a peach pie."

Nikhil had keenly observed his significant role models working and heard the term *work* used often enough to apply it accurately to his own experience. We adults were intrigued by the power of example and felt challenged to uphold role models worthy of Nikhil's imitation.

Early Childhood: Work as a Task and an Activity

Already in early childhood (0–6 years), the child is capable of appreciating that the child's work—*play*—is a task and an activity that captures interest and engages focus. The enthusiasm and enjoyment of play also extends to the performance of simple household *chores*. Knowing that his parents need his help and trust him to accomplish a task, Nikhil looks very self-satisfied each time he puts his books back on the shelf or the trash in the trash bin; these simple assignments have already become a natural part of his routine.

Play as Work

In the last century, Maria Montessori, renowned Italian physician and educator, appreciated the importance of play in a young

4

child's life and referred to play as the "work" of the child. Play is not a frivolous and aimless flutter of activity. Montessori asserted that play, when geared to the age level, capacity, and interest of the child, helps to normalize the child, i.e., to calm and focus the child and satisfy his energy and curiosity. Montessori believed that the young child has an absorbent mind, which, when purposefully engaged, has a capacity for disciplined work When the child understands the activity and instructions and has teaching materials that meet the child's natural appetite to learn, then play helps the child to develop the mind from within and builds self-reliance and independence. [1]

I can give firsthand testimony to Montessori's astute educational philosophy and methodology. All four of our children attended a Montessori *Casa* or preschool for three- to six-year-olds.

Yearly, the school administrators and teachers planned an open house and invited parents to observe their child for one hour "at work." With four offspring, I had the pleasure of many observations over a span of ten years. Although my attention focused essentially on learning abilities and behavior, I also welcomed the opportunity to observe each child's socialization. Supplied by the teacher with well-constructed guidelines for observation, I knew what to look for but was in for some surprises. These are my impressions of our children's work, as observed during each child's first year in preschool at the age of three.

Our firstborn, Christine, started and completed eight activities within the hour. With focus, precision, and drive, she plunged into her work. She was learning the economy of efficiency and how to be task-oriented. A self-starter, she knew what she wanted to do and how to do it. Today, as a corporate executive, she brings these same qualities to her position.

Cindy, our second child, started and completed only one activity, the arduous task of arranging color tablets in gradation, going from the darkest to the lightest. She chose an activity that develops color appreciation and visual harmony. In the process, she was learning the scientific method, an orderly progressive approach to work. Today, she tackles her work in research and clinical practice with the same logic, thoroughness, and determination.

Third-born Ricci started an activity, then stopped several times for some momentary mischief and playfulness (like hiding a classmate's material under the chair), before he continued with his task. I wondered if he would find in the Montessori environment an outlet for sustained attention. He soon did and settled into an activity that totally absorbed his concentration and restored calm. He was learning how to channel his energies. Today, he works in the corporate world where his street smarts and sense of humor are assets.

As our youngest son, Anton, approached his tasks, he did the unexpected. Instead of using the teaching materials according to the teacher's instruction, e.g., building a tower of blocks, he went one step beyond and constructed a tower blindfolded. He appeared to find most joy and satisfaction when he was able to experiment. He was learning to explore untried paths and perspectives. Today, he works in film and photography, and as a DJ, where he applies his creativity and "out of the box" thinking.

Over the years, I have come to appreciate Montessori's conviction that play is a preparation for work and self-discipline, a forerunner for developing good habits or virtues. Observing our children at "work," gave me glimpses of their developing dispositions toward work, let alone their individual temperaments and personalities. Many other theorists of progressive preschools, who have incorporated purposeful play into their methodologies, affirm her insights. In unison, they recognize cardinal developmental needs of the child: *eagerness to learn* and *willingness to do*, and rightfully advocate starting children at a young age.

The Work of Toys

While professional educators offer expertise and teaching materials carefully chosen or specifically designed to meet the learning needs of the child, parents rely on toys to develop the child's potential. In a consumer society, they are bombarded by a mind-boggling array, perhaps with little time to discern the benefits and advantages of each. Eager to give the child a head start in a competitive world but skeptical about the senseless toys that get piled in a closet, caregivers are encouraged to consider several criteria in their choices of toys in early childhood.

Marylou and Fred related, "We decided to take Sandra with us to the toy store to see what would catch her attention. Then we would have a better idea about what to buy for her birthday. Well, *everything* caught her eye, but we did make some interesting observations. Push-button toys that simply required Sandra to switch the toy on and off to make it perform did not sustain her interest. At home, we have noticed that play dough, puzzles, housekeeping toys, playing cards, drawing, coloring or painting sets, dolls, puppets, and balls sustain her involvement; hands-on toys that help her understand cause and effect or develop independence are the best. And she loves construction-type toys that help her build something."

"What about stuffed toys?" I asked.

Sandra has a favorite stuffed toy, her dolly; they're inseparable, especially at bedtime. But her other stuffed toys are on display and tend to be dust collectors.

Well-meaning gift givers at a birthday party are often dismayed by the very young celebrant who seems to show much more interest in the box, wrapping paper, and decorative string or bow than the expensive toy that tends to provoke passivity instead of focused activity. More appropriate in early childhood are toys that stimulate *learning by doing*, i.e., manipulation, discovery, exploration, imagination, organization, classification, comparison, inquiry, discernment, and creativity.

Willie had crossed bridges many times on his way to visit cousins, but today he decided to build one on his own with his *Legos*—small, colorful plastic bricks. At first he approached the task through trial and error, but at least he was generating his own experiences. Along the way, he appreciated some suggestions or guidance, especially when he was stumped or frustrated. What he did *not* want, however, was a well-intentioned parent, caregiver, or sibling who would take over and build the bridge for him. Willie experimented, manipulated, and eventually learned how to do the job in an increasingly methodical way. With unhurried time and minimal interruptions, he was tapping his energies and developing coordination and stamina; he was learning to concentrate, think independently, and persevere from beginning to end until he built his own bridge. These are the makings of good work and of a competent, confident worker. In time, as Willie progresses towards more complicated constructions, he will engage in more systematic learning, develop dexterity, and cultivate a sense of accomplishment.

Opportune Moments contains suggestions that guide parents in the art and craft of helping the child in early childhood to understand the meaning of work.

Opportune Moments

To help the child understand the Meaning of Work in Early Childhood (0–6 years)

- Refer, on occasion, to the child's play as *work* to help the child equate the two.
- Listen to the child as he talks about play, chores, and activities. Ask questions.
- Talk about your own work or task at hand in a spontaneous and natural way; give explanations of what you are doing. If possible, arrange for an occasional (or regular) work-from-home schedule.
- Tell stories about people at work, especially people whom the child knows.
- Read books about workers and their jobs such as a fireman, truck driver, teacher, doctor.
- Select television programs and videos that feature people at work, e.g., the neighborhood mailman, or things at work, e.g., Thomas, the train engine.
- Limit total viewing time of up to a maximum of two hours per day for the child of three years and above. Implement rules on media usage consistently (see chapter 4).
- When time allows, especially on weekends, seek alternative activities to media usage, e.g., arts and crafts, sports, excursions, imaginative games, dancing lessons, learning to play an instrument.

Cont'd.

- Foster physical activities to develop motor control, coordination, and dexterity.
- Carefully select toys that meet the child's interest and inner need to learn, build, imagine, and gain control over himself. Avoid those that provoke passivity and only short-lived usage.
- Patiently explain and repeat instructions for a new toy or material.
- Show interest in the child's play even if the child repeats the same activity.
- Take time to play with the child and enjoy playtime together!
- Check with the child's school to find out the subject matter the child is learning; try to reinforce the ideas through storytelling and reading.
- Establish close home–school collaboration.
- Assign simple chores to children between the ages of 2½–4 years, capitalizing on the child's eagerness and willingness to do them, e.g., pick up toys, clothes, and books and put them in their proper places; throw soiled clothes in the hamper; help get a toy or diaper for a baby sibling; dress self.
- Coordinate with the child's day care, preschool, or school to identify the tasks or chores that the child is learning to do; make these part of the routine at home. If a nanny helps care for the young child or the child is in day care, explain the need to follow through on chores.

Cont'd.

- Between four to six years old, add other chores, e.g., fix bed; help clean up own room; fold towels and clothes; pack school bag; water plants; care for a pet; set table.
- Explain, demonstrate, and repeat how to do the chore.
- Encourage the child in progress; give positive encouragement and feedback; repeat often.
- Involve the child spontaneously in new chores as the occasion arises, e.g., put groceries in the closets or pantry after a trip to the market.
- Consider and with moderation carefully select out-of-school activities to expand the child's experiences and socialization, e.g., soccer, karate, Daisy Scouts, T-ball, ballet, wrestling.

ROLE MODEL the naturalness of work!

Middle Childhood: Work as a Process and Duty

As the child matures into middle childhood (ages 7–12), he moves beyond the idea of work as play. Work evolves into a process and duty, undertaken in studies, chores, and activities, e.g., chess and checkers, sports, band, orchestra, school newspaper or yearbook. At home, the child may need to decipher the rules of a computer game, or he may plunge into a labor-intensive hobby entailing considerable perseverance and study. Our youngest, Anton, and his best friend, Timmy, carefully painted their model soldiers and created dioramas of battlegrounds. Their work was based on research of famous battles and became the forerunner of long discussions in adolescence about possible film scripts, which they hoped to produce some day!

Complaints, obstinacy, tedium, or dissatisfaction may set in as the child studies for a quiz or completes an assignment that he finds difficult or useless. But study has the potential of becoming more satisfying than play, especially if it taps into the creativity of the child. If study is interspersed with satisfying alternative activities that supplement and diffuse the intensity of homework, the child thrives from the good product mix.

Whether he is a member of a team or group activity that depends on his participation or must simply button the coat of a baby brother, the child begins to recognize that there are assignments that must be accomplished and procedures that must be followed because they help others.

Practical guidelines to direct the child in middle childhood follow in *Opportune Moments.*

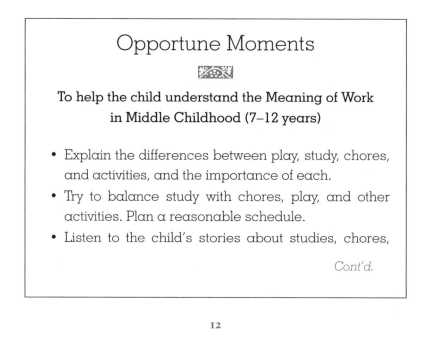

Opportune Moments

**To help the child understand the Meaning of Work
in Middle Childhood (7–12 years)**

- Explain the differences between play, study, chores, and activities, and the importance of each.
- Try to balance study with chores, play, and other activities. Plan a reasonable schedule.
- Listen to the child's stories about studies, chores,

Cont'd.

hobbies, sports, music. Ask questions, show interest, and monitor the impact of each.

- Share interesting, amusing anecdotes about personal experiences at work, whether at home or at the workplace, to reinforce bonding in the parent–child relationship.

- Bring the child to your workplace for a look-see or to watch relatives, friends, or neighbors at work.

- Encourage questions; ask about the child's impressions of different kinds of work and the people who undertake it—their qualifications, why they chose this job, and how they do it.

- In casual conversation, facilitate the realization that study and achievement are partners—study makes possible the attainment of objectives.

- Explain the meaning of study and what it entails: understanding objectives of an assignment; techniques to accomplish it; consequences of studying. Offer feedback and help, as needed.

- Give the child opportunities to do increasingly complex chores, e.g., sort out recyclables for pick-up; help a younger sibling with homework; help prepare dinner; help rake leaves; put laundered and folded clothes in drawers and closets; walk the dog.

- Explain that with increasing age come increasing responsibilities, especially school assignments. The child needs to understand that not everything he does will be fun and games. In learning to persevere

Cont'd.

and sustain effort, he is better prepared for the more serious work ahead.

- Express appreciation and encouragement of the child's participation in chores.
- Explore interests and special talents of child in the form of hobbies, e.g., collections.
- Be realistic about individual capabilities and make appropriate provisions for each child.
- Encourage participation in extracurricular activities based on the child's aptitudes, interest, and willingness.
- Resist overloading the child with too many activities or chores that may exhaust the child and interfere with studies. Together with the child, establish a reasonable balance that gives the child joy.
- Carefully monitor media usage, sensitive to the positive and negative impact of prolonged exposure. Be vigilant and exercise caution and control, especially of violent programs and those that debase human sexuality (see chapter 4).
- Curb parental expectations and competitiveness.
- Set an example of doing work with joy and the spirit of sacrifice.

ROLE MODEL conviction and perseverance in work as a necessary means to attain a goal.

Adolescence: Work as a Challenge and an Opportunity

If the groundwork of work as play, study, chores, hobbies, and activities has been laid, the teenager comes to view work as a reality of life, something to be dealt with daily. He now has a choice: he can undertake work as a challenge and opportunity or as a burden and source of oppression. The decision is within the teenager's control. The actual task at hand may, in fact, be difficult and exhausting, but if undertaken with a sense of its importance, it can be a source of satisfaction and fulfillment.

Challenges are plentiful for a teenager in the twenty-first century. Take Jasmine, Noah, and Ted. Each copes with chronic information overload from cyberspace and multimedia usage. With worldwide political instability as a daily backdrop, each teenager confronts more immediate personal problems or issues affecting work and study. Jasmine's behavior evidences dysfunction in her family; she juggles studies with too many extracurricular activities just to avoid going home. Noah cautiously talks about experiencing peer pressure to try drugs; he is trying to balance an after-school job with homework. Ted admits logging in regularly to pornography to escape from stress; he is overwhelmed by the college admissions process and parental expectations.

Challenges can be converted into opportunities. For instance, diligence and perseverance could translate into acceptance at the university of choice or even a scholarship! As the adolescent matures and internalizes work-study with conviction, he begins to appreciate work as a self-imposed duty that must be undertaken with a sense of responsibility. In the process, he is bound to attain a greater sense of accomplishment. Laziness, on the other hand, could have costly short- and long-term consequences.

Perceptive teenagers, who have observed effective role models, gradually deduce that work is ongoing and a lifelong undertaking that may have many forms and variations in the course of one's life. With maturity comes the realization that work—whether done well or poorly executed—will have long-term effects.

Opportune Moments offer suggestions to reinforce the understanding of work among adolescents.

Opportune Moments

To help the child understand the Meaning of Work in Adolescence (13–19 years)

- Continue to monitor, encourage, and follow up the teenager in studies. Try to spot those subject areas that engage the teenager's interest and enthusiasm, tap into specific talents and skills, challenge the teenager's creativity.
- Show interest in classmates, hobbies, sports, and activities, girl/boyfriends. Keep the lines of communication open.
- Listen to the teenager's voluntary comments, observations, and insights about study and work.
- Elicit the adolescent's thoughts about the meaning of work, i.e., its importance, challenges, consequences.
- Encourage part-time jobs, internships, or summer

Cont'd.

jobs, e.g., as a babysitter, caregiver of the elderly, waiter, clerk, salesperson, lifeguard. Experience strengthens attitudes, habits, and appreciation for the value of hard work.

• Follow up on chores to help the teenager follow through. Chores could include things like participation in laundry, meal preparation, gardening, car care, shopping for groceries, cleaning, polishing floors, cleaning the car. Decide on how to "reward" the worker, e.g., allowances, special privileges, or a simple thank you!

• Continue to encourage the pursuit of sports, music, or hobbies as a means of developing self-discipline. Despite the generation gap—e.g., in musical taste— try to understand and support the teenager's interests. Do some research to keep updated. Network with other parents.

• Continue to monitor multimedia exposure and be vigilant regarding its effects (see chapter 4).

• Guide the teenager to discern goals, future career choices, and job opportunities.

• Encourage or arrange to meet workers at the workplace to expose the teenager to potential careers, the realities of the job and its organization of labor, the implementation and impact of technology in the particular field.

• To develop a balanced perspective and help the individual strengthen against setbacks and disappointments, paint a realistic picture of the difficulties,

Cont'd.

monotony, and stress at work, as well as the joys, satisfaction, and rewards.

- Discuss causes and consequences of work poorly done, including laziness, graft, and corruption.
- Ask the teenager to try to envisage the positive long-term effects of good work on personal and family life, community and national development, and the nation's cultural heritage.

ROLE MODEL satisfaction, fulfillment, and perseverance in work as a reality of life and lifelong vocation.

Attitudes toward Work

Understanding work's meaning lays the foundations for doing work. When the child understands the activity at hand, he grasps its essence; when he realizes the reason for doing it, he appreciates its importance. The "what" and the "why" give focus and impetus to work and are cornerstones of attitudinal formation.

Attitudes are points of view or more persistent dispositions; they contribute to a frame of mind. Attitudes towards work are already in the making in the very young child whose senses are keen and alert as he absorbs the world around him.

Attitudes may be positive or negative, certain or skeptical, rigid or flexible. Although they are basically stable dispositions, they are not necessarily fixed and permanent. They may change or take several directions over a period of time, depending on a host of variables that influence the child: thoughts, interpretations and motivation, emotions, experiences, skills development, special circumstances, role models, or environmental and cultural values and practices. Following are several examples of the dynamics of attitudinal formation.

When Danny, a consistently eager student in middle school, began suffering severe bouts of asthma and prolonged absences, he experienced academic setbacks. He became demoralized and shunned studies for most of the school year. His attitudes toward school were very negative until a patient, understanding teacher redirected him. When Patty, a new student, experienced social isolation from her peers, she became preoccupied and distracted and couldn't concentrate on her studies despite having previously been a good student. She was able to restore good study habits only after she made friends. When Jay made the high school varsity football team, he was aware that staying on the team would require maintaining good grades. Although he hadn't taken studies very seriously before, now he was highly motivated to get better grades and started to approach homework assignments with greater focus and commitment. Wisely, his parents encouraged and reinforced his efforts. He became a valuable team player and he continues to apply his positive attitudes through conscientious study habits in college.

For twenty years, Noelle, Lara, Mariel, Christine, and Cindy watched us mothers, Melinda and myself, roll out the dough for cookies, listened to our conversations about preparations and plans for the holidays, smelled the gingerbread cookies baking, and helped decorate the cookies with colorful frostings and decorations. They were undergoing attitudinal formation in the setting of the home through the seemingly ordinary work of baking cookies. During our annual bake-off, the children were exposed to images and messages about work: the fun and socialization of working together in the labor-intensive, creative task of serious cookie making. As their artistic skills increased year by year, we mothers observed that our daughters felt challenged to design new shapes and produce works of art. By adolescence, their creations looked too good to eat, and we actually took photos of them before savoring their taste. To my delight, the bake-off continues as an annual family tradition, proof of very stable dispositions that had already begun forming in the preschool years.

As the primary educators and role models of children, parents and caregivers contribute tremendously to work attitudes. Children really do live what they learn; they assimilate criteria, first based on what they see as example and then through gradual discernment. If Mommy returns home from work persistently short-tempered and frustrated or Daddy often arrives angry and complaining, then young children may get the impression that the parents' workplace is a terrible place that promotes unhappiness. They may think of ways to avoid work in the future. Of course, parents do have "bad days" and unwittingly voice their grievances; things that happen only occasional are not likely to give rise to long-term negative attitudes. The sensitive, vigilant parent tries to put the grievances in context so as to help the child understand the realities of work. This requires considerable parental self-discipline and patience.

It also can happen that when a parent spends many hours away from home trying to make ends meet, the child may not perceive the self-sacrifice involved. He or she may actually resent parental work until mature enough to appreciate family financial circumstances. Other potentially negative attitudes toward work may develop if parents or caregivers do not allow the child to participate in work, especially in household chores. If, for example, a well-meaning nanny prevents a young child from doing tasks and taking responsibility for what is done, the child is likely to become complacent and timid and to lose confidence. When others chronically take over and do things for the child, they prolong dependency. The child loses opportunities to empower himself and develop skills and fortitude.

Working parents, Phil and Kathy, pampered and spoiled their youngest daughter, Annie. They exempted her from any household duties and shielded her from their own childhood experiences of hard work. At seventeen, Annie commented in a conversation with her friends, "Household chores are so demeaning!" Phil and Kathy had miscalculated the effects of their childrearing, including the potential long-term negative attitudes toward work they were engendering in their child.

On the other extreme, Suzanne, the eldest in a family of four children, was assigned all of the responsibilities during her parents' long hours at work. She told her friends how much she resented the duties imposed on her. "Work is like a curse and punishment!" she exclaimed. Suzanne's parents had not distributed the chores in a reasonable, equitable manner among their other children who were capable of doing some of the work. They, too, had provoked negative attitudes towards work and working.

The development of attitudes in children is always a work in progress that relies in part on the caregiver's input, example, and appropriate childrearing strategies.

Habits at Work

Good habits or *virtues* predispose a person to seek truth and to do good. When the behavior associated with a good habit is performed naturally, promptly, easily, and willingly, it empowers and enables the attainment of self-actualization. Among the habits that motivate good work are industry, diligence, punctuality, order, fairness, and self-discipline.

The particular virtue that helps a child grasp the *meaning of work* is essentially understanding. It fosters appreciation of the art and science of work. Little Nikhil, busy working on his jigsaw puzzle, has a long way to go in the formation of good habits related to work, but if he is continually guided in his attitudes to view work as something joyful, understands the task at hand, perceives it as worthwhile, follows instructions, finishes the activity, and returns his toy or material to its proper place, the foundations of virtues are being laid. He is off to a good start!

The opposite of a virtue is a *vice*—a much easier habit to develop! Vices are habitual defects or shortcomings developed over time that dispose a person to corresponding bad behavior. Negative habits contrary to good work include laziness, tardiness, irresponsibility, disorder, unfairness, lack of self-control, and dishonesty.

"Tiger, have you finished your homework?"

"Yes, Mom." But, in truth, nothing had been done.

Two days later, Tiger's mother learned in a note from his teacher that her son had failed to submit several assignments. Increasingly concerned about Tiger's dishonesty, his mom realized the need constantly to check and redirect a habit that had probably begun because Tiger hadn't previously gotten caught lying or had gotten away with it so often that it had become a vice.

Problems in the Process

Even among the best-prepared or most experienced parents or caregivers, difficulties are likely to arise when trying to foster the child's internalization of the meaning of work in play, study, chores, hobbies, and activities. These difficulties can include the child's lack of interest, opportunities, experience or exposure, boredom, distractions, confusion, discouragement, and disorder.

Caregivers themselves may face problems because, although well intentioned, they are misguided in their efforts. Among the possible problems are lack of time, preparation, parenting or communication skills, and ineffective role modeling.

To help in resolving problems related to the child's understanding of the meaning of work, basic childrearing strategies that may assist the child, parent, or caregiver in getting *Back on Track* are discussed in chapter 4.

For Reflection

1. *"This process of working is universal: it embraces all human beings, every generation, every phase of economic and cultural development . . . whereby man 'subdues the earth' through his work."*[2] Any thoughts to add?

2. What *Opportune Moments* have you successfully implemented? What other strategies would you suggest to caregivers?

3. Cite an example of good role modeling that you have set to help the child appreciate the *meaning of work*. What improvements can you make?

4. Think of a specific resolution you can make to help the child understand the *meaning of work* better.

Chapter 2

THE PIE FACTORY:

The Purpose of Work

PAPA'S FIRST JOB

"Papa, tell us again. You know, the story about the pie factory!" Loretta and I pleaded to hear about Papa's first job in the United States.

Personal circumstances had compelled Papa to migrate from Germany to America in 1927 before the Depression. With only one semester to go to finish work for his engineering degree, he had taken a big risk in leaving Germany without it. He was never able to work as an engineer in his new homeland. Instead, he was a tool and die maker for fifty years.

A mischievous smile was followed by a chuckle as Papa recalled the memory.

"I arrived in the New York harbor. *Vat* a beautiful lady *velcomed* me . . . the Statue of Liberty! I *vas* very happy to greet her.

"*Onkel* Julius met me at the pier. He *varned* me of the difficulties—almost impossibility—of finding *vork* quickly, so I decided to start my job hunt immediately.

"At sunrise, the next morning, I *valked* from one factory to another. All I could see were signs, 'Not Hiring' and 'No Openings.' I tried to apply at every company, but each *von* turned me down. I *vas* almost ready to give up, *vhen* in late afternoon I saw a sign, PIE FACTORY. I didn't even know what the *vord* pie meant.

"The foreman *vas* a German immigrant like myself. He asked me to show him my hand. 'You're in luck, Freddie,' he said. 'You have the right size hand. You can start tomorrow.'

"I was so happy and relieved. *Vhen* I reported to work, the foreman gave me a pair of rubber gloves, apron, and cap. After a short training period, I *vas* ready to start. There *vas* an assembly line. Small, round aluminum pie tins, *vhich vere* lined with pie crusts, came along very quickly on a conveyor belt. I had to dip my hand into a barrel of apple pie filling and carefully pour *von* handful of filling into each pie crust."

At this point, Papa demonstrated his movements.

"*Vhen* I finished with the apple pies, I started with barrels of blueberry and cherry filling. That *vas* my job. That's how I earned a living."

❀ ❀ ❀

Seeing our delight, Papa told the story each time with gusto. We children, of course, were amazed that our Papa could fill pies at such a fast clip!

The job was short-lived, however. One morning, as Papa was coming out of the factory after completing the night shift, his fellow workers beat him up. They wanted to teach him a lesson. Apparently his work was held up as a benchmark for the other workers to follow. Reluctantly, the foreman laid him off for fomenting unrest! Not deterred, Papa found another job, this time as a stevedore on the New York docks, before he finally found more permanent employment.

In time, his financial circumstances improved considerably. Somehow, Papa always managed to find work and, I'm sure, rendered a good day's service in every job. To his credit, in ten years' time—by 1937, that is—he had purchased a car and a small, modest house. Then he sent for Mama, who sailed the Atlantic to marry her childhood friend, whom she hadn't seen in ten years!

As far back as I can remember, Papa also held to a work-study regime. English dictionary in hand, he learned five new vocabulary words every evening after dinner during his leisure; in between, he often sketched designs and inventions. At seventy-one, he started to teach himself French, because he wanted to take Mama on a second honeymoon trip to Paris!

For Papa, family always came first. He sacrificed with extraordinary humility and love.

Fast Forward

Seventy-six years after Papa first saw Lady Liberty in New York Harbor, grandson Ricci in 2003 faced the same job search dilemma, only now there were search engines to do some of the walking. People with MBA degrees had been in popular demand by corporate recruiters for many years, but now there was a decline in jobs for them. It took many months before Ricci, degree in hand, found suitable employment. Meanwhile, he held temporary jobs, including driving a truck of props to film shoots. With graduate school debts and monthly rent to pay, Ricci realized, "I know what *Opa*"—'Grandpa' in German—"went through," and he took courage from his grandfather's example.

The Economic Dimension of Work

Spanning generations, grandfather and grandson confronted the most basic dimension of work—the economic one. Even with the best of intentions and eagerness to work, Papa and Ricci faced a reality: the need to earn a living versus the unavailability of jobs. They managed to find employment, but they took jobs requiring less than they had in the way of qualifications. No matter. Both were thankful for the income and the chance to work.

Asked, "What is the purpose of work?" during Work Attitudes Seminars I have conducted in corporations and academe, the first reaction among participants is always "to earn a living," followed quickly by "to support a family." These are natural responses to humankind's quest for survival and a dignified, humane standard of living.

The economic dimension of work covers a wide spectrum of human experiences and attitudes, from preoccupation with sheer survival to obsession with the lifestyles of the rich and famous.

Supporting a Family in a Consumer Society

In a free market economy and consumer society like the United States, what it means to earn a living and support a family in the twenty-first century is far removed from what it may have meant to parents in an agricultural economy of centuries past, when children worked side by side with them in the fields and assumed adult responsibilities at an early age.

Today, whether parents are providing for a family in an urban setting or in rural America, families face an incredible array of consumer products in shopping malls, department stores, discount outlets, boutiques, and bazaars crying out from the shelves, "Buy me! Buy Me! You can't live without me! You can't be happy without me!" Expectations of material comfort and acquisition have risen. Artificial needs have been created. Families often are lured into lifestyles of consumption unheard of in many parts of the world. They work hard to buy into the "American dream." And, once there, they work even harder to sustain it.

The modest "American dream" that Papa and Mama pursued has evolved for some into an obsessive quest for wealth. Unrelenting in their pursuit, some parents think of little but making money and lose sight of other nobler dimensions and purposes of work.

Parenting in a Consumer Society

During an International Family Congress held October 2004 at the United Nations, the keynote speaker identified two of the greatest enemies of parents in the twenty-first century. Expecting to hear complex analyses, the audience was surprised when he simply named *fatigue* and *lack of time* as the culprits.[1]

Eager to provide for the family, parents make hard choices and sacrifices. In a dual working arrangement, mother and father both arrive home tired, even exhausted. With only limited time to spend with their children, they are overextended. They find it difficult to balance career and family life. Playing Super Mom or Super Dad after a day of work outside the home is overwhelming. Playing Super Mom or Super Dad as a stay-at-home parent can be equally demanding. And playing the role of sole breadwinner as a single or solo parent places extraordinary demands on the caregiver. Parents often feel out-of-control, or guilty, or frustrated. They may be tempted to take the easier way out and exercise *permissive indulgence*. This is a parenting style that fails to set parameters and structure and spoils children with material goods. Overwhelmed by technology in this multitasking generation, each member of the family may operate independently from the other. One may be on the cell phone, another in a chat room, another playing a computer game, and still another watching a video. Little time is allotted to family life and the development of family relationships. Some parents simply give in or give up, while failing to perceive the downside to their neglect. Well-intentioned as she was, Laura, a working mom, overcompensated every payday by buying Tommy and Elena the latest videos and computer games. It became a routine. At the end of the month, the children waited at the door for their reward!

The impact and influence of high technology, multimedia, and the entertainment industry cut across socioeconomic levels, from the highly affluent to struggling immigrants. Parents and children alike are bombarded with an information overload shaping values and attitudes that may run counter to respect for work. Children are fueled by advertisements and pressured by peers who remind them daily of the goodies they can't live without! Already, five-year-old Margie had begun to compare her belongings and toys with those of her preschool classmates. At home she whined and cajoled her parents until she wore them down and they bought her what she wanted.

Nine-year-old Reggie promised his parents he would get all A's on his report card, if only they bought him more games for his PlayStation! His classmates were putting pressure for more games for their GameCube or XBox.

By adolescence, the need to belong is strong and conformity to peer pressure peaks. When fifteen-year-old Melissa set out to buy a pair of jeans and faced an array of slim fit, easy fit, relaxed fit, baggy, extra baggy, stone-washed, acid-washed, button-fly, zipper-fly, faded, or regular from which to choose, she felt pressure. "What do I really need and want? What style suits me? What color is best? What is the current fashion?" Then she had to answer the pivotal questions: "What are my friends wearing? What will my friends say?" The freedom to make a simple choice had been complicated by so many options, although the moment of truth came with a glance at the price tag. The blue jeans of her choice were beyond her budget. Melissa asked the same series of questions over again until she reached a compromise choice.

The moment of truth came to Lee when her daughter Tammy, in grade four, nagged her for a cell phone. Lee decided she needed to make hard choices and weighed the pros and cons. She inquired among other parents and finally decided that the distraction and cost of the cell phone were simply too great.

Paul and Peggy asked themselves crucial questions when their son Michael, a sixth grader, demanded an iPod.

"What have we been working for? What kind of example have we set, that Michael should feel he has the right to ask for such an expensive item without meriting it?"

For Peggy and Paul, the more disturbing issue was their son's attitude of self-righteousness and entitlement. Clearly, the effects of the "good life" had crept in subtly, and the expectations it engendered had become the standard for him. The hard-working parents had a serious talk with Michael, disclosed relevant facts about the family budget, and encouraged him to save his allowance and cash birthday gifts to pay for what he wanted. Parenting is not for the fainthearted. It never has been, but today parents can be overwhelmed or derailed from their parenting goals. Consider the topics that parenting organizations and parent–teacher associations have asked me to speak on lately during conferences and seminars: "Parenting in a Consumer Society," "Permissive, Indulgent Parenting," "Developing Resiliency in Children," "Effects of Multimedia on Children." The topics mirror parental concerns and their eagerness for answers to the bottom-line question:"Is too much of a good thing a good thing?" And if not:"How do we deal with this good thing which has spiraled out of control?" When children get the impression that shopping, acquisition, and accumulation of goods are the main goals in life and that the primary purpose of parental work is to sustain this lifestyle, they have missed out on the delight of knowing a Papa and *Opa* who loved work and proclaimed its nobility through example.

Of course the *economic* dimension of work includes positives: earning a living, supporting a family, contributing to the economic prosperity of the nation. But parents may find themselves sidetracked by economic concerns from the other dimensions and purposes of work that enable, ennoble, and empower the worker as a whole person: the *personal, social,* and *ethical dimensions.*

The Personal Dimension of Work

Through work, the worker fulfills a basic need to learn and engage in purposeful behavior. Struggling to develop talents and capabilities, a human being realizes personal potentials. When work is done to the best of individual ability, self-actualization is attained.

The Social Dimension of Work

At and through work, the worker renders service to others and fosters relationships through which he may help another attain individual purposes and goals. Work is the vehicle that unites humankind—families, communities, and nations. Working collectively, workers develop teamwork, promote the common good of society, and contribute to the cultural and technological heritage of the nation.

The Ethical Dimension of Work

Work's true value lies not just in output and profits, but essentially in the human person who can enhance human dignity and integrity through upright ethical decisions and the practice of work-related virtues. In the process of working, the worker may face dilemmas that require the discernment of truth and goodness in order to uphold ethical standards.

Early Childhood: A Need to Learn and Do

Energy, exuberance, and curiosity characterize early childhood. On the go from morning until night, caregivers of young children often find themselves exhausted in their efforts to keep up.

For Tommy, who built a tower and then knocked it down with glee, and Ginny, who asked her Daddy to read her the same story over and over again, and the twins, Rhoda and Rhona, who ran races with their parents until the latter were ready to drop, their activity—essentially, play—was perceived as fun. Children like the feeling of purposeful behavior and socialization. Work comes easily to the spontaneous young child whose curiosity makes him open to learning. In time, the child finds that with understanding, obedience to instructions, and self–control, play gets done even better.

Opportune Moments present strategies and early foundations for guiding the young child to relate to the multiple dimensions and purposes of work.

Opportune Moments

To help the child understand the Purpose of Work in Early Childhood (0–6 years)

Economic Dimension: To help the child understand the appropriate use of money

- Reserve gift giving for special occasions, e.g., birthday, holidays.
- Resist the child's demands and pestering for toys and/or the temptation to compensate for absences by buying extra rewards.
- Avoid creating material needs for the child through "impulse buying"; let the child observe how purposeful, necessary purchases are made.
- Encourage the child to save coins in a piggy bank or open a savings account.
- Economize by using hand-me-down clothes, toys.

Cont'd.

Personal Dimension: To help the child learn and act with purpose

- Identify those activities, toys, and books in which the child finds satisfaction and focus. They will give a clue to the child's interests, aptitudes, and individual talents.
- Once they are identified, encourage repetition of these play and reading activities to help the child focus, direct energies, and maximize learning experiences.
- Create opportunities and occasions that encourage learning in a natural, spontaneous way, e.g., family outings, excursions.
- Encourage or lead the child to articulate what he has done or learned. Let explanations come from the child, e.g., about a drawing, painting, story.
- Gradually introduce the why of play and chores. Give simple explanations. By the age of 3½–4 the child should be able to explain why he is doing something.
- Exercise parental media management and guide the child to discern what he is watching or playing (see chapter 4).

Social Dimension: To help the child develop and strengthen relationships

- Play with the child; enjoy and share in the child's enthusiasm.
- Thank the child for participation in chores.

Cont'd.

- Encourage the young child to help care for the youngest in the family.
- Encourage mixed-age group play (3–7 years), but avoid play with older siblings in win-or-lose games or situations.
- Expand the child's social circle by inviting playmates or classmates over. Be sensitive to different temperamental types. Some children may be very sociable, while others may warm up slowly to new experiences or settings.

Ethical Dimension: To help the child develop good habits or virtues

- Patiently help the child to develop good work habits: joy in doing something well, understanding of the process or procedure, obedience to parent and caregiver, self-control, order.

ROLE MODEL joy in learning and purposeful work.

Middle Childhood: Development of Competence and Confidence

By middle childhood, increased experience and multimedia exposure have propelled the child into the world opened up by his imagination, curiosity, concern, endless questions, and even worry. Whereas in years past children tended to play more outdoors, and girls collected dolls while boys collected cards or model airplanes, in today's generation of media babies Joanna, Bob, and John text messages on their cell phones, download music to their iPods, and engage in social networking on their computers' "MySpace" or "Facebook." They may spend their leisure comparing, tracking down, and trading computer games.

When they return to the real world, Joanna, Bob, and John find that homework isn't as much fun as media diversion and chores can't be done by pushing a button. Nevertheless, as they exercise self-discipline and acquire competence, they grow in confidence. Competence and confidence build healthy self-respect and a more secure base for relationships with family, friends, and classmates. They are fortified by the practice of virtues, e.g., diligence, responsibility, patience, perseverance, generosity.

Some tips to promote a better understanding of the purpose of work in middle childhood follow in *Opportune Moments*. Lessons learned in each dimension facilitate the right dispositions toward work in adulthood.

Opportune Moments

To help the child understand the Purpose of Work in Middle Childhood (7–12 years)

Economic Dimension: To help the child understand the value of money

- Avoid spoiling and indulging the child with a constant flow of material rewards and the latest hi-tech gadgets. Learn to say no and give clear, definite explanations.
- Establish a policy on allowances: fixed, or fixed

Cont'd.

allowance dependent on completion of chores, or no fixed allowance with money given on a need basis. Once established, consistently follow the policy. Be specific about amount, conditions, and limitations.

- When shopping with the child, explain criteria for selection of goods and purposes of purchases.

Personal Dimension: To help the child develop competence and confidence

- Encourage initiatives and independence of thought in studies. Avoid reliance on others, e.g., tutors, unless in the case of illness. Offer the appropriate assistance, when needed.
- Guide the child in the gradual process of gaining mastery in skills.
- Encourage and praise the child's efforts in all work endeavors, e.g., studies, chores, school activities, hobbies, sports, music.
- Offer suggestions for improvement in a positive tone, avoiding name-calling and accusatory, blaming, humiliating put-downs.
- Let the child take responsibility for his own work.
- In casual conversation, ask the child what the benefits of work are. Use this as a springboard for conversation about the multiple dimensions of work.

Social Dimension: To help the child function in a group and be of help

- Actively engage the child in family activities like family

Cont'd.

meetings, excursions and trips; assign responsibilities, e.g., help plan the trip, help pack the suitcase and snacks.

- Join the child in multimedia usage; exercise caregiver media management (see chapter 4).
- Encourage family communication to teach the child the art of discussion, problem solving, compromise, and negotiation.
- Encourage participation on teams and in community-based programs.

Ethical Dimension: To fortify the child's responsibility toward good work

- Provide occasions for the practice of work-related virtues: self-discipline, diligence, responsibility, patience, perseverance, generosity, determination.

ROLE MODEL joy, self-discipline, moderation, and creativity in work.

Adolescence: Enhancement of Self-Actualization, Identity, and Independence

Adolescence is characterized by changes in all domains of development. These are the years of growth spurts, mood swings, insecurities, critical thinking, idealism, vulnerability to peer pressure, and cultural and moral sensitivity. The developmental changes impact on the teenager's attitudes toward work, study, and chores.

Capable of understanding the multidimensional purposes of work, the adolescent confronts the need for some serious decision-making. He may embrace work and through it foster self-actualization, enhance identity and individuality, develop independence, and experience a sense of accomplishment. Choices in favor of good work will require consistent effort in acquiring and exercising the virtues of sound judgment, fortitude, service, justice, accountability, and courage. On the other hand, the adolescent may choose to avoid, evade, manipulate, or reject work, and for these choices, too, he must take the consequences.

Several years ago, I received an invitation from a Montessori school to conduct a Work Attitudes Seminar with its third- and fourth-year high school students. We started with a brainstorming session that required the students to enumerate the reasons why they work. Their responses paralleled those of adult corporate seminar participants! I was duly impressed with the depth and breadth of the teenagers' appreciation of work and the issues they raised, e.g., study habits, professionalism, love of learning, future careers, job opportunities. In the course of our discussions, they admitted that they found more satisfaction in working than in "hanging out" and doing not much of anything. *Why* wasn't I surprised? The Montessori principles, methods, and materials that develop a natural love for work from the earliest years had done their job.

In comparing the purpose and value of the school custodian's work with that of the principal's, we concluded that *title and job description were secondary to the importance of the worker as a human being, his good intentions, and the quality of work done.* The students admitted that they found joy and excitement in learning and in their work. In Montessori's own words, through work "what resulted was not just the child's happiness, but the child began his work of making a man. Happiness is not the whole aim of education. A man must be independent in his powers and character, able to work and assert his mastery over all that depends on him."[2]

At the close of the seminar, we reviewed the basics of work and summarized its function and purpose.

Function and Purpose of Work

- a dynamic, universal process of humankind
- any decent, meaningful human activity
- a challenge to apply knowledge and skills
- a task undertaken intentionally, freely, responsibly, and seriously
- a means to an end
- a chance to transform the object of work and give it greater value
- an opportunity for improvement and self-actualization
- an opportunity to care for the environment
- a channel for service to others
- a means to build strength through the practice of virtues
- a personal effort to build a better world

Opportune Moments

To help the child understand the Purpose of Work in Adolescence (13–19 years)

Economic Dimension: To help the teenager spend money wisely

Cont'd.

- Encourage a part-time or summer job so as to have the experience of earning a livelihood.
- Give the teenager tips on how to budget money and minimize expenses.
- Encourage savings!
- Avoid giving the child a credit card or establish a very firm policy about its use.
- Demonstrate the art of bargain-hunting and the advantages of sales.
- Help the teenager set priorities and keep needs simple, i.e., not to follow fads and whims, even if money is readily available to pay for them.

Personal Dimension: To help the adolescent attain self-actualization

- Guide the teenager to see him/herself realistically, i.e., talents, aptitudes, maximum potential.
- Help the teenager set realistic objectives and goals based on an objective self-assessment.
- Encourage standards of excellence relative to individual capabilities.
- Encourage the teenager to start and finish work in whatever form—e.g., studies, chores—despite hardships and setbacks.
- Suggest tips for good time management to maximize productivity in work and the effective use of leisure.
- Guide the teenager to establish a realistic balance among study, chores, hobbies, sports, music.

Cont'd.

Social Dimension: To help the teenager learn how to work well in a group and contribute to the common good

- Foster family solidarity through a spirit of mutual help and sharing. Be sensitive to symptoms of egoism, competition, and manipulation among siblings and get at the root of the rivalry.
- Take time to explain how a single family member can affect all the members adversely and undermine the good of the whole.
- Encourage cooperation and responsibility towards other family members. Create opportunities for teenagers to help the very young and very old members of the family.
- Encourage participation in neighborhood activities, outreach programs, and volunteer work to expand the teenager's socialization with others in the community.

Ethical Dimension: To help teenager strengthen ethical decision-making

- Guide the teenager to value moral uprightness in work.
- Give opportunities to practice virtues, e.g., sound judgment, fortitude, service, accountability, courage, justice.

ROLE MODEL simplicity, honesty, consistency, and perseverance in work.

Problems in the Process

Problem situations related to helping the child appreciate the multiple purposes of work arise when the child experiences the distractions of a multimedia environment and a consumer society, or lacks explanations, guidelines, structure, opportunities, encouragement, or training.

Parents and caregivers may contribute to problems by engaging in permissive, indulgent parenting, setting a poor example, or through a lack of time, patience, experience, or energy to deal with the challenges. (See *Back on Track*, chapter 4, for basic parenting strategies to deal with adverse situations.)

For Reflection

1. *"Work is a witness to the worth of the human creature. It provides a chance to develop one's own personality; it creates a bond of union with others; it constitutes a fund of resources; it is a way of helping in the improvement of the society we live in, and of promoting the progress of the whole human race."*[3] Any thoughts to add?

2. What caregiver strategies have you found most helpful in counteracting the effects of consumerism?

3. Cite an example of good role modeling that has helped the child appreciate the multiple *purposes of work*. What improvements can be made?

4. What specific resolution can you make to help the child understand and respect the *purpose of work* better?

Chapter 3

MY GIFT:

The Value of Work

PAPA'S SECRETS

"Papa, Papa. Please tell us again. You know, the story about the pie factory." For the nth time, Papa satisfied his daughters' request, but this time his story took a new turn.

As always, he described the scene of the pie crusts hurrying along the conveyor belt and demonstrated his job of filling the pies.

Noted for my sweet tooth, I couldn't resist asking a question, "Papa, did you get to taste the pies?"

He chuckled and said, *"Ja!"* but he added that his taste for apple, blueberry, and cherry pies was short-lived after daily immersion in the odor of the fillings!

Loretta, more practical and perceptive, asked, "Did you ever spill the filling? Didn't you find the job boring?"

Papa's face took on a more serious expression.

"*Vell*, maybe I spilled a little, but only rarely. Boring? No! Not at all. You see, I looked at my job this *vay*. God gave me the gift of life. I *vanted* to say 'thank you' and offer him a gift in return, so I offered my gift of *vork* every day. I had many pies to send up to heaven. That's why I *vas* very careful not to spill any filling. I wanted to give God beautiful pies, not ones that looked sloppy. I *vanted* to give others a gift too, a pie that looked appetizing."

※ ※ ※

Papa's secrets were out! With his simple explanations, he had revealed the true motivation underlying his positive attitudes towards work. He elevated his work to the divine and wanted to be of service to others. His explanations made lots of sense to us children: here was an honest day's work performed for noble reasons.

Papa had grasped several profound insights, which he transmitted to us children, about the value of work as a gift. Finding a way to bypass the toil and monotony of labor, he understood that

> the legitimate pride of doing work well relieves it of much of its drudgery. Some people, who have held on to this craftsman's standard, get a thrill from any job they do. They know the satisfaction of a "job well done" whether they are caning a chair, cleaning a horse's stall or carving a statue for a Cathedral. Their honor and self-respect are heightened by the discipline of careful work. They have retained a whiff of the Middle Ages . . . Labor was not then merely for the sake of economic gain, but through an inner compulsion for excellence . . . projected in human effort.[1]

Workers derived their sense of honor and dignity from the quality of the work they did and its service to the common good. Their lives were at once enriched and strengthened through work, and their souls were refreshed. Like Papa, they looked beyond the economic dimension to find inspiration for work.

Fast Forward

In a highly industrialized consumer society that extols output and consumption, how is work perceived? Do workers still hold on to a craftsman's standard and "get a thrill from any job they do?" Do they find genuine value in work?

Research points out the paradox of work today. "On the one hand, 84 percent of American men and 77 percent of women say they would continue to work even if they inherited enough money so they no longer needed a job."[2] These findings clearly suggest that work is valued as something worthwhile, a disposition that likely develops early on.

"Already in the first year of life, infants show pleasure in causing events, as when turning a tap or a light switch on and off, or knocking a ball suspended over the crib. Children in a reasonably stimulating and structured environment learn to enjoy concentrated effort. Indeed, our species would not have survived if most of us had not developed a taste for work."[3]

But there also are contradictory data. The inconsistency may be partially explained by a materialistic mindset conditioned to expect and prefer a lifestyle of comfort and leisure without work.

"Ironically, most people who work experience a more enjoyable state of mind on the job than at home. At work it is usually clear what needs to be done, and there is clear information about how well one is doing. Yet few people would willingly work more and have less free leisure time . . . Generally unnoticed is the fact that the work we want to avoid is actually more satisfying than the free time we try to get more of."[4]

Extensive studies in the *psychology of flow* over the past two and a half decades shed light on satisfaction in work. The research affirms that satisfaction can be derived from absorption in a task like work. When the worker sets goals, finds a balance of personal talents and challenges at a task, is able to focus and concentrate energies, and develops a sense of mastery, he peaks in his abilities and performance. He experiences an "optimal experience" or *flow* and finds direction, strength, and happiness. In so doing, the worker enhances the quality of his life through the intensity and joy that he experiences.[5]

For caregivers, the challenge to foster *flow* begins in early childhood when the child is open and receptive to beginning the process and cultivating the value of work.

Early Childhood: Discovery and Care of Nature

The very young are the most open to the marvels and wonders of nature. They are in awe of insects, flowers, colorful autumn leaves, rocks, and babbling brooks that they see. But animal life elicits even greater amazement. Hours before leaving for the zoo, Sara and Joe were eagerly anticipating which animals they would see. They wondered if they would be allowed to feed or touch, as in "show and tell" at preschool. Hardly able to contain their excitement, they wanted to visit the pet store on the way home. And once at home, they likened themselves to the zookeepers as they fed their fishes and turtles.

Amazed by the size of giant trees, the strangeness of sea creatures, the immensity of dinosaurs, the remoteness of the moon and stars, the child intuitively respects those who care for the environment or work to discover more about the universe.

Fascination with nature and the cosmos, reinforced perhaps by television—e.g., *Animal Planet, Discovery Channel, National Geographic*—or videos, the child explores planet Earth and beyond. He learns about forest rangers and park caretakers as well as rocket scientists and astronauts, and the importance of their work.

This is an opportunity to explain humankind's responsibility to help maintain nature's balance and protect the environment. Chores at home that elicit the young child's early accountability for nature are most often greeted with willingness and enthusiasm, and the young child attaches value to these tasks.

Habits and attitudes related to the value of work start early and can take different directions. The child may develop an appreciation for nature or he may manifest disregard and neglect. He may show good manners toward all workers or express disrespect. Human beings are free, after all, and their freedom can be acted out in ways that are bad as well as good. Early groundwork provides a good start in virtue-building, but continuous practice and encouragement are necessary just the same.

More recently, psychologists who subscribe to *positive psychology*[6] emphasize the importance of "traits that promote happiness and well-being, as well as character strength such as optimism, kindness, resilience, persistence, and gratitude. These positive characteristics, sometimes called character strengths or even ego strengths by psychologists, will be recognized by members of all major religions and by most philosophers as names for what used to be called the virtues."[7] In fact, they are still called virtues by these people and many others, and it is good to know that psychologists now are reaffirming—by whatever name—the exercise of good habits that put positive work attitudes into practice.

Hints in *Opportune Moments* help guide the child in early childhood to appreciate the value of work and the worker.

Opportune Moments

To help the child understand the Value of Work in Early Childhood (0–6 years)

- Inspire and facilitate the child's exploration of nature in the environment and appreciate its wonders through visits to parks, forests, farms, mountains, beaches, and other such settings.
- Help strengthen observation skills by guiding the child to distinguish colors, sizes, shapes, names of leaves, seeds and pinecones, flowers, birds, etc.
- Explain how different plants attract other creatures like bees and worms, and how all have a role in nature.
- Help the child value all forms of life including even the "creepy crawlers," but also caution the child about real dangers like bee stings and snake bites.
- Teach the child to be thankful for the gifts of nature.
- Give opportunities to plant seeds, care for a pet, help in the garden.
- Explain the importance and urgency of caring for and protecting the environment.
- Train the child to show good manners and respect to workers who care for animals and the environment, e.g., zookeepers, forest rangers, farmers, street cleaners, as well as those who explore and study planet Earth and the cosmos such as scientists, researchers, and laboratory technicians.

Cont'd.

- Challenge the child with games: a "what would happen if . . . " game to help them see the devastation that nature and the environment would suffer if planning and care are neglected; or the "blindfolded guess game" allowing them to touch and feel natural objects, e.g., tree bark and leaves, and then guess what it was they touched.
- Train the child to clean up his own mess and exercise civic responsibility, e.g., not to throw, crumble, or break materials, or discard them indiscriminately.
- Explain how wastage or lack of care spoils the environment, e.g., destruction of forests, contamination of water sources.
- Demonstrate how to prolong the use of materials and/or recycle old toys and materials to counteract a "throw-away" mentality.
- Train the child to care for personal possessions and help others care for their belongings.
- Train the child to respect the possessions of others, ask permission to use another's property, and show appreciation for being allowed to use it.
- Include among birthday gifts educational toys that teach about the world, e.g., globe, books, jigsaw puzzles of animals or nature scenes.
- Remind the child to say "thank-you" for gifts.
- Motivate the practice of virtues: gratitude, obedience, respect, order, appreciation, kindness, caring, patience.

ROLE MODEL the mindset of a grateful environmentalist who cares for nature and the welfare of all workers.

Middle Childhood: Mastery of Skills and Service to Others

In the middle years the value of work to the child expands considerably as he takes his first big reality pill. He is now more conscious of his stake in nature and the environment and increasingly aware of happenings at school, in the community, and in the world. Further tasked with school assignments and involvement in activities, the child has an inkling of what is expected of him: work!

If he is to keep up with studies, chores, hobbies, and activities, he must gain competence and mastery. To achieve mastery requires guidance and help; but beyond receiving comes the duty of giving. Internalizing the qualities of a good citizen means that the child must participate, be accountable, and help others for the benefit of the greater good of the group.

All of these components of building character converged during a recent field trip of public middle school students to a science museum. I had the pleasure of chaperoning the excited, spontaneous children, who delighted in the wonders of nature. They squealed when they were allowed to touch a snake, were astonished when they saw bees at work, marveled at the displays in the oceanography, astronomy, and energy rooms, all offering hands-on activities.

Still goofy and giggly, the children exhibited the range of sizes and shapes typical of pre-pubescence. They bought silly souvenirs like dinosaur hats in the museum gift shop. Although mostly preoccupied with the here and now of their own jokes and laughter, their questions reflected curiosity and some serious scientific inquiry. Perhaps there were great scientists of tomorrow among them.

At lunchtime in a fast-food restaurant, they shared not only food but impressions of their exhilarating museum visit. Then they cleaned up their tables and returned to their seats in the bus, careful to check on the whereabouts of their assigned partners. Throughout the day, they were respectful of the teacher's authority and instructions.

These youngsters were thrilled to have a day off from schoolwork, but they were clearly happy and satisfied as they cheerfully worked to acquire greater understanding of the universe they live in, an increased realization of its complexity, a heightened awareness of their role in exploring and caring for the Earth, greater participation and cooperation skills, sensitivity in caring for the welfare of others, and growth in the ability to make responsible use of the freedom given them during the field trip. As a culminating school activity, the excursion showed that lessons in work had been well learned.

Among the students on the field trip was one twelve-year-old who stood out in the group: the ice skater. She was an exceptional example of a child in middle childhood who had found value in her work: mastery of skills and a spirit of service. Janet had already won ice skating championships that reflected daily morning and afternoon practices, before and after school. Her achievements inspired and propelled her to perfect her art and craft and aspire to new heights. Best of all, she really loved the sport and found her turf, her *flow*. Her classmates admired and respected her talent, self-discipline, and fortitude. She took the admiration in stride, quick to admit that she was up against stiff competition in the next contest that would surely test her mastery of techniques and grace under pressure. As an honor student, she was ever willing to help tutor her classmates.

Opportune Moments consolidates suggestions for caregivers of children in middle childhood.

Opportune Moments

To help the child understand the Value of Work in Middle Childhood (7–12 years)

- Encourage the child to plant and cultivate, if possible, a plot or small garden of fast-growing plants or herbs, e.g., oregano, instead of using store-bought products.

- Give simple science lessons in the setting of the home to help the child apply principles that have been learned, e.g., by explaining and using certain foods that have medicinal properties, such as garlic, ginger, and chilies, or by adding home-grown oregano while cooking spaghetti sauce.

- Continue to encourage the child's exploration of nature by such means as conversation, hobbies, and media programs.

- During visits to supermarkets or farms, help the child connect certain foods with their natural ingredients, e.g., multi-grain bread.

- Encourage participation in projects that enhance the environment, e.g., community waste campaigns.

- Remind the child to give continuous thanks for the gifts of nature.

- If the family budget allows, plan day trips, weekend excursions, camping trips, or summer vacations that put the child in touch with nature and elicit his participation in caring for the environment.

Cont'd.

- Encourage the development of talents, hobbies, sports, or music that require practice and self-discipline.
- Create opportunities to practice competencies and develop mastery in academic subjects, hobbies, sports, or music. But be careful not to overextend the child's energy, stamina, and capabilities.
- Encourage the child to share talents with others.
- Guide the child to maintain a balance between schoolwork and leisure pursuits, planning for cycles of activity and relaxation.
- Give reminders about chores in a manner that is firm yet creative and humorous.
- If the child complains, remind him how work builds character.
- Encourage the practice of virtues: industry, responsibility, self-discipline, cooperation, honesty, fortitude, service, generosity, and cheerfulness.

ROLE MODEL perseverance, steadfastness, quality, and joy in work.

Adolescence: Enhancement of Dignity and Integrity

By adolescence, work acquires a serious character. Depending on the teenager's attitudes, work can become a channel leading toward achievement and service, or an unfortunate requirement and mundane nuisance. It can be an occasion for the exercise of virtues by upholding ethical principles or of vices by shortcutting professional ethics. A choice is necessary—to do work in a manner that enhances dignity and integrity or to take a less honorable route.

Eva chose the latter. Assigned to a group term paper in her high school history class, she felt lucky, because her group was composed of the class geeks who would surely do outstanding work. This would be a "no-brainer" and easy way to get a high grade. What she didn't count on was the clever distribution of tasks and topics that the group members had planned, meant to ensure that each one did his fair share.

The self-proclaimed "Miss Laziness" momentarily panicked until she remembered that her cousin, an honor student in another city, had tackled the same topic in a paper and was willing to share it with her. The rest was simply a mechanical matter of downloading the paper and choosing the appropriate passages to submit as her work. Eva missed out on an opportunity to learn and participate. Instead she chose the path traveled these days by some students: the quick fix of plagiarism.

Her decision was a costly one, because her teacher immediately spotted the discrepancies between her previously submitted assignments and "her" newly acquired writing style. She paid the price of failure and lost the chance to prove her capabilities and find satisfaction in her efforts.

Through her unwillingness to uphold the value of work, Eva demeaned herself by not applying her learning potential and talents. In submitting plagiarized work, she betrayed the trust of her teacher, cousin, and classmates. Mostly, she failed to uphold ethical standards. To the disappointment of her group, she did not exercise her responsibility like the others who were eager to learn, work together, and produce good work. Eva had made a mockery of work and diminished her own integrity and dignity.

In contrast, the members of Eva's group approached the assignment with a zeal for discovery and focused their joint commitment. Through the group activity, Eva's teacher was training her class in the attributes of a professional who seeks excellence in work. The project was a training ground to develop the mindset and good habits that are demanded of anyone who sets out to attain and sustain a high standard of work, no matter what the position or title.

Thus "professional" and "professional work" as used here do not refer only to doctors and lawyers and the like and the kind of work they do. "Professional" means someone who does work of any sort—blue-collar workers, agricultural workers, housewives and mothers whose work is done in the home, and volunteers of all kinds. Whoever the worker is, and whatever the form of work he does, professional work is work done according to the highest standards of that sort of work.

A professional is not an obsessive-compulsive, fanatical perfectionist or workaholic. Rather, he is one who prioritizes his tasks; sets realistic expectations; organizes and manages time well; communicates effectively; delegates when necessary; works diligently; plans, foresees, and follows-up. These competencies are not beyond the reach of maturing adolescents. With more training and opportunities in similar class undertakings, Eva's classmates were developing a sense of professionalism and making responsible use of the freedom given them in the group project. They were empowering themselves toward self-development, self-achievement, self-improvement, and self-management in preparation for adult professional work.

Eva failed to use sound judgment, which would have required foresight, insight, and hindsight. She missed out on a potentially valuable experience and instead decided in favor of vices instead of virtues. *Flow* is a more likely side effect with the practice of the good habits of self-respect, prudence, persistence, courage, honesty, conviction, commitment, resilience, empathy, service, and optimism. In a highly competitive environment, several scenarios may play out. A teenager like Eva may get the impression that one gains a competitive edge by doing whatever it takes to gain it. By observing and imitating overly ambitious role models who have forsaken ideals, the teenager concludes that work ethics are reduced to manipulation and deception devoid of values. Winning is everything, even at the price of human dignity. On the other hand, the diligent teenager may get confused and question why honest, hard work oftentimes goes unrewarded, while unscrupulous performance is extolled. Demoralization, even cynicism, may set in. Or adolescents who are pitted against classmates in a highly competitive school setting may get the message that the only goals are to compete and succeed, not learn. Or siblings whose parents habitually make critical comparisons between them may feel discouraged, especially if they try hard but are labeled or ridiculed instead of encouraged and inspired.

Caregivers of teenagers face a particularly serious and sensitive challenge: *to strengthen the maturing adolescent's moral foundation that empowers him to opt for ethical standards and uprightness in work.* They must transmit the invaluable message of work's nobility: *the value of work is rooted* not just in acquiring and winning, but *in upholding human dignity and ethical standards, producing quality performance, and providing service to others.* At the end of the day, it is the Papas and Mamas of this world who demonstrate to this generation of workers the honor and self-respect of disciplined work.

Opportune Moments provide suggestions to the caregiver of an adolescent.

Opportune Moments

To help the child understand the Value of Work in Adolescence (13–19 years)

- Continue to promote the mindset of an environmentalist who is aware of issues like chemical pollution and toxic waste.
- Encourage the teenager to write to local councilmen or government officials on vital environmental issues, e.g., segregation of waste, recycling.
- Encourage good environmental citizenship through participation in advocacy projects and community efforts such as cleaning graffiti off of walls.
- Remind the adolescent about the care of the body as a necessary prerequisite for effective, productive work by nutrition, exercise, sports, hygiene.
- Continue to encourage the teenager's efforts and mastery in study, chores, hobbies, and activities with a mix of encouragement, praise, inquiry, advice, and allowing personal space.
- Emphasize the need for sound judgment and consequential thinking to gain insight, hindsight, and foresight in work.
- Foster and facilitate accountability for personal behavior, the responsible use of freedom, application of ethical standards, and excellence in work.
- Seek feedback from teachers about the quality and

Cont'd.

integrity of the teenager's schoolwork, if necessary inquiring into issues like cheating and plagiarism.

- Get feedback from the school about the teenager's socialization, e.g., participation in activities, circle of friends, manners.

- Encourage participation in group experiences like the school play, newspaper, or yearbook to gain in socialization skills, spirit of service.

- When the opportunity arises, cite examples of professionalism among family, neighbors, colleagues.

- Monitor the teenager's expenditures, concentration in studies, peers, and changes in behavior, especially if addictions are suspected. Seek professional counseling as needed.

- Provide opportunities to practice the virtues of self-respect, prudence, persistence, courage, conviction, commitment, resilience, empathy, service, and optimism.

ROLE MODEL the self-respect of a professional who produces quality work and upholds ethical standards.

Problems in the Process

Special problems may surface when helping the child understand the value of work. They may concern sensitive issues like the dignity of the human person, ethical judgments at work, the development and application of work-related virtues, environmental concerns, or effective and consistent role modeling. Basic childrearing strategies that can be applied to problem solving are suggested in chapter 4, *Back on Track*.

For Reflection

1. *"I long to accomplish great and noble tasks, but it is my chief duty to accomplish humble tasks as though they were great and noble. The world is moved along, not only by the mighty shoves of its heroes, but also by the aggregate of the tiny pushes of each honest worker."*[8] Any thoughts to add?
2. How do you explain to a child the importance of caring for the environment and showing respect for the dignity of workers regardless of job, position, title, or prestige?
3. Cite an example of good role modeling you have set for professionalism at work. What improvements can you make?
4. What specific resolution can you make to help the child appreciate the ethical standards of a professional?

Chapter 4

KIDNAPPED:

Media at Work

PAPA'S TELEVISION RULES

Papa and Mama panicked when I was not home by 6 for dinner. It was already 7:30 p.m. and Esther, 9, was missing, and probably kidnapped!

They called the police. The siren alerted the entire neighborhood. When the police car stopped in front of our little white house, everyone was deeply concerned. Meanwhile, Mrs. Mangano, our next-door neighbor, ran to her second-floor porch to check out the scene. She had been busy cooking in the kitchen and hadn't noticed that I was watching a cowboy movie on her television in the living room with her children. With Papa and Mama at work, I had gotten into the habit of going next door to play with Chickie and Frankie and watch TV. In the early 1950s we were the only family in the neighborhood who didn't own one.

The event profoundly affected us all. I was devastated to see the look on my parents' faces and know that I had caused such anguish. They were horrified to think that I might have been lost forever. Grounded for weeks, I learned my lesson, and I guess they did too. Within a few months, we were the proud owners of our first television set.

We followed four basic rules that Papa had decreed: only he had the privilege of turning on the TV; no daytime viewing was allowed because that is the time when people work; a minimum of 2–3 persons had to watch the program or else it was not economically feasible, a waste of electricity; and definitely no cowboy movies could be watched! He found the latter much too violent.

⊠　⊠　⊠

And so the family that watches TV together stays together! Most Saturday evenings the Joos family could be seen watching the *Lawrence Welk* show!

Fast Forward

Half a century later, the issue of media exposure must be met head-on by parents who are raising a high-tech child in an information society. With the availability of television, movies, CDs, DVDs, Internet, video, and computer games as regular and convenient babysitters, media have become guest members of the family—to be welcomed, but with caution and vigilance.

Given the goal of fostering understanding, attitudes, skills, and habits related to work, caregivers are challenged to ask some bottom-line questions.

Bottom-Line Questions Related to Media Exposure

- Is exposure to media a meaningful, worthwhile activity for the child?
- Is using media a good use of the child's time and developing talents?
- How does media viewing or interaction enhance the development of understanding, attitudes, skills, and habits related to the work of the child, e.g., play, study, chores, hobbies, activities?
- How can the parent/caregiver best exercise control and media management to maximize benefits to the child?

Early Childhood: Children's Television and Developmental Media for Infants

Significantly, in 1999, the American Academy of Pediatrics issued to pediatricians recommendations that "pediatricians should urge parents to avoid television viewing for children under the age of two years. Although certain television programs may be promoted to this age group, research on early brain development shows that babies and toddlers have a critical need for direct interactions with parents and other significant caregivers for healthy brain growth and the development of appropriate social, emotional, and cognitive skills. Therefore, exposing such young children to television programs should be discouraged."[1]

Extensive research findings on the effects of visual media on children are readily available through Internet search

engines. To date, studies appear to focus more on the nega-
tives, e.g., aggressive behavior, perhaps because of the alarm
and skepticism voiced by child psychologists and psychiatrists,
family therapists, educators, guidance counselors, parents, and
clergy who observe adverse effects in children. Because of
the relative newness of computer technology, studies that cite
long-term effects are less available. In contrast, prominent
children's television programs that are targeted for the very
young have been well documented. Following is a small sampling of studies that reflect both the strengths and limitations
of media.

- *Sesame Street*, a pioneering children's educational television
  series of the Sesame Workshop, formerly Children's Television Workshop, by 2006 had produced more that 4,000 epi-
  sodes since it began in 1969, with the original televised in
  120 countries.

- First- and second-grade school children who had watched
  Sesame Street as preschoolers were more likely to read story-
  books on their own and less likely to need remedial reading
  instruction.[2]

- Already in 1971, teachers more often rated *Sesame Street*
  viewers as well adjusted to school. Thirty years later, in a
  similar study, teachers made the same observation.[3]

- In a "recontact" study, high school students who had watched
  educational television as preschoolers, *Sesame Street* in particular, had significantly higher grades than nonviewers in
  English, math, and science in junior high and high school.[4]
  Another longitudinal study indicated that the students also
  used books more often, showed higher academic self-esteem,
  and valued academic performance more.

- *Blue's Clues*, another children's program targeted for pre-school children presenting a simple, predictable format that invites interaction, fosters school readiness.[5]

Notwithstanding positive learning and reinforcement that children have received from media, parents are encouraged to keep the number of viewing hours and the kinds of programs viewed under their careful control and guidance in order to ensure that the child experiences a balance of work, media, and socialization with others.

Other studies indicate limitations, unreliability, and contradictions, if not detrimental impact on the part of visual media.

- With increasing competition from other children's programs and critiques of *Sesame Street* that described the show as a "disjointed series of animated flash cards" of "inherent blandness and triviality" with a "curriculum that focuses on mere technical skills,"[6] the Sesame Workshop research department re-examined fundamental principles and re-evaluated the program design. They reformatted the program geared to a growing number of younger viewers and included more predictable modules, a simplified number of characters, and fewer interruptions.

- Concerned with environmental factors that may put the child at risk for attention deficit hyperactivity disorder (ADHD), a study of seven-year-olds who had experienced early television exposure suggested that the number of hours of television viewed per day at both ages one and three was associated with attentional problems at age seven.[7]

- One study showed that 46 percent of all television violence took place in children's cartoons, and these were least likely (5 percent) to depict the long-term consequences of violence. Violence is portrayed in a humorous fashion 67 percent of the time.[8]

- Although mothers may give testimony to the calming or distracting effects of developmental media for babies (e.g., *Baby Einstein, Baby Mozart*), no reliable research supports claims made for the benefits of the baby videos. A product of the Walt Disney Company, the videos present gentle, free-form images of babies, toys, etc., with music and words. [9]

In early childhood, the caregiver assumes a dual role—a filter screening out useless or misleading programs, and a co-viewer interacting and giving explanations or commentaries to guide the child. If the major activity in the day of a young child is entertainment via indiscriminate and unsupervised exposure to media, the child is deprived of meaningful work-play. The example of prudent parental selection, participation, and self-discipline is imperative if media are to be allies rather than obstacles in childrearing.

Middle Childhood: Television, Computer Programs/Games, and Advertisements

Unless the use of media is kept under control, diversions and distractions from work-study are likely occurrences in middle childhood. Research studies pay special attention to the impact of media during the ages of 7–12 because of the increasing vulnerability of the child to visual images and interactive play. On the positive side:

- Neural processing exercises disguised as computer video games are being used successfully to reduce the impairment of dyslexia.[10]

• "Starbright World" is a computer network that helps seriously ill children cope with loneliness and isolation by linking hospital pediatric units and giving the children opportunities to interact. Another of its programs helps children recovering from chemotherapy to escape into imaginary worlds, thus relieving anxiety, pain, and stress.[11]

Studies show that the amount of time spent playing computer games peaks in the years from middle childhood to early adolescence (grades 4–8). Boys play computer games more than girls at all ages.

• Girls prefer cartoons or violent games with fantasy themes whereas boys prefer more realistic games featuring human violence.

• The conclusions of studies of the effects of violent games vary widely, from no measurable effects or minimal effects, to desensitization to violence, including decreased empathy and strong pro-violent attitudes, and increased feelings of hostility and aggression.

• Some children are in a "high-risk" category for aggressive behavior.

• Substantial but varying dependence or addiction to games has been reported among children who begin playing at younger ages.[12]

As for television viewing, research shows such effects as these:

• A fifteen-year longitudinal study (1977–1992) of boys and girls ages 6–10 found that those at most risk of engaging in aggressive behavior in young adulthood had been exposed to television violence in childhood, had identified with aggressive television characters of their own sex, and perceived television violence as realistic. Parental co-viewing and commentary on programs are suggested to reduce the effects of television violence on children, as well as use of V-chip technology to give parents a way of controlling what can be broadcast in the home.[13]

• In a school-based trial involving nine-year-olds given lessons on decreasing television viewing over a six-month period, the children had significantly decreased levels of body fat, and ate meals in front of the television far less often, compared with children not in the program.[14]

Advertising is another media force bombarding caregivers and their children. More than $12 billion was spent on advertising and marketing to children in 1999, almost double the amount ten years earlier. In 1968, consumers younger than twelve spent $2.2 billion; by 1998, the figure was $23.4 billion.

Parents need to keep a close eye on media exposure in middle childhood. Habits form at this stage. If a child by temperament already predisposed to violence is regularly exposed to media violence without supervision or control, the short-term result could be playground bullying, and difficulty participating and cooperating in class, socializing with classmates, or doing studies and chores. In the long term, anger and defiance may someday spell the difference between a worker who is cooperative and productive and one who is disruptive and inefficient.

Media management is a vital responsibility for caregivers. The following guidelines may be of help. Prevention is more effective and efficient than intervention after things have gotten out of control.

Guidelines for Media Management

- Screen media programs for content, values, age appropriateness, language, and quality of production. Check out rating systems.
- If possible, take a computer course and become familiar with what is available online.
- "Test-drive" computer games to assess the amount and kinds of features, imagery, violence, and sexual content.
- Install protective computer software that filters out potentially harmful content.
- Set rules about media use by the child. Explain these rules. Be specific and definite about the kind of program, place, time, duration of usage, and day of the week.
- Consistently enforce the rules.
- Monitor and follow up media use.
- Co-view with the child and comment on programs to minimize the effects, especially of violent programs. Elicit the child's reactions, thoughts, and perception of the reality of the program. Redirect faulty perceptions.
- Plan satisfying alternative activities to keep the child from overexposure to media. Participate and enjoy the activities with the child. This includes things like excursions, imaginative games, sports, arts and crafts, and reading.
- DARE TO SAY NO when programs or games are

Cont'd.

offensive or a waste of time and attention. Turn off the television set, or switch channels, or remove the computer game from circulation, or relocate the computer to a public place in the home.

- Try taking a family break from media and engage in family activities instead. Just see the results!
- Network with other parents to get feedback or exchange suggestions about worthwhile programs and computer games. Participate in advocacy programs or information campaigns, e.g., anti-pornography, consumer rights, children's rights. Join campaigns against cyberspace crimes against children.

Adolescence: Television, Videos, and the World Wide Web

Computer technology has brought about an extraordinary information explosion requiring workers to be well prepared for the demands of a knowledge-based economy. With the availability of excellent educational programs and the World Wide Web, teachers and parents gratefully recognize numerous heightened opportunities for children to acquire valuable information, ideas, and skills. At the same time, however, they are understandably concerned about the fact that children and adolescents have neither the innate ability nor, in many cases, the training in critical thinking to be able to deal with the information overload.

When a teenager consults a search engine and finds that there are 26,323 available research studies relating to his homework assignment, where does he begin, how does he discern, and when should he stop? And, sheer volume aside, it is even more crucial that he be able to distinguish and make judgments between what is relevant and irrelevant, moral and immoral, necessary and unnecessary, worthwhile and useless.

At this stage of development characterized by increased hormonal levels and interest in sexuality, the adolescent is further intrigued or enticed by the large number of Web sites and television programs, films, and videos featuring sexual content.

Several research studies conclude that American television shows portray largely unrealistic, unhealthy, suggestive sexual behavior, sexual innuendoes, and vulgar four-letter words on prime time.

- Seventy-five percent of shows on the major networks during prime-time TV contain sexual content, but only ten percent of the incidents include any mention of the risks and responsibilities of sexual activity.
- Sexual suggestiveness in the media has increased dramatically during the last two decades, according to studies.[15]
- There has been a steady increase in venereal disease among young people as a consequence of adult-like sexual activity.[16]
- Several studies indicate that adolescents likely overestimate the number of their peers and friends who are sexually active and are likely to feel more pressure from media than from friends to begin sexual relations.

Of concern is the child's exposure to pornography, whether intentional or in the course of media browsing.

- In 2000, a congressional study of Internet use found that one out of four children seventeen or younger had stumbled across pornographic pictures while surfing the Web.

71

- In a study of 600 American male and female students of junior high school age and above, 91 percent of the boys and 82 percent of girls admitted having been exposed to hardcore pornography. Over 66 percent of the male students and 40 percent of the female students reported wanting to try out some of the sexual behaviors they had witnessed. Among high schoolers, 31 percent of the male students and 18 percent of the female students admitted actually imitating some of the things they had seen in the pornography within a few days after exposure.

- In a study of 932 sex addicts, 90 percent of the men and 77 percent of the women reported that pornography was significant to their addiction.

Although parents and caregivers are likely at times to feel that they have lost control of the situation while raising adolescents, they should not relinquish their role as authority figures. If parental media control is begun in early childhood, chances are good that the child will internalize parental expectations and role modeling, positive values, and reasonable self-regulation.

However, a multitude of factors can delay or hinder the development of healthy attitudes towards sexuality. These include emotional maladjustments, peer pressure, academic setbacks, or the impact of a dysfunctional family. If such factors are reinforced by exposure to pornography, the teenager may be influenced or predisposed to experiment and engage in unhealthy sexual behavior or develop a sexual addiction.

Caregivers need to give serious consideration to—and frequently act upon—suggestions like these: vigilance of the child's attitudes, behavior, routines, and friends; installation of filtering devices to screen out objectionable Internet content; parent and child discussions—without sermons; explanations derived from ethical-religious beliefs; serious and realistic warnings about the consequences of sexual practices; firm household rules about computer use; and professional counseling and therapy if unhealthy or deviant sexual behavior is suspected.

Serious preoccupation with sex is likely to prevent the adolescent from concentrating on studies, growing in emotional stability, and experiencing healthy socialization. The ability to do good work either now or in the future may be badly impaired. In the adult workplace, sexual addiction and sexual harassment have become major corporate headaches, subjects of lawsuits and recovery programs that have resulted in enormous losses in profits, work hours, and morale.

Back on Track

In our less than perfect world, things have a way of going wrong. Despite their enormous beneficial impact, media are powerful forces that have unanticipated effects on children, parents, and the parent-child relationship. More than half a century ago, I was one of the first victims of television's power to "kidnapped" children. Entranced by the TV images, I found I could escape into worlds beyond imagination. And now an unknown power, which they viewed with a mixture of awe and fear, confronted Papa and Mama: television had introduced new dynamics into our relationship.

Although Papa's TV house rules may have been extreme, he foresaw the need to manage this invasive houseguest. Caregivers who have observed a major change for the worse in a child's attitudes or behavior related to media usage know the anguish this can cause and how important it is to help get the child back on track.

Little Eileen, only three and a half, was mesmerized by her favorite television programs and videos, several of which were inappropriate for her age. She had tantrums when she didn't get to watch them. Mom Sandra coped as best she could as a well-intentioned solo parent, but she admitted that she relied heavily on a babysitter and media to keep Eileen distracted and obedient. How can caregivers help a child like Eileen?

Or what about Preston, age ten, who retreated into his own world of computer games in preference to playing with friends, doing school assignments, and participating in family life. At first, Preston's parents were relieved to see their shy son immersed in such a time-consuming, fascinating hobby. In time, though, they became alarmed at his increasing isolation and aggression. What can his parents do for Preston?

What about Celeste, fifteen and curious, longing for some special attention? The chat room became her retreat into companionship and flattery. At the other end of the connection was Mr. X—not the shy, cute, seventeen-year-old high school basketball player Celeste envisioned, but a forty-six-year-old predator who knew exactly how to tap into adolescent insecurities and fantasies. After gaining her trust, he suggested that they meet. Before the date, he e-mailed her seductive photos to show the kind of clothing he wanted her to wear for their first meeting. Celeste's parents, who hadn't set rules or limitations about surfing the Internet or chat rooms, noticed subtle changes in her behavior. She seemed preoccupied and secretive and couldn't concentrate on schoolwork. What can parents do to rescue a teenager like Celeste?

To say the least, what Eileen, Preston, and Celeste were doing was clearly not conducive to the development of good work attitudes and habits. They channeled their interests and focus elsewhere, while avoiding work at hand, e.g., study, play, chores, and activities. At a time when they should have been actively engaged in purposeful work, they escaped into full-time media. In this and other ways, these children were headed for serious trouble.

Parents who have faced similar situations know the anguish their caregivers felt. Patterns of behavior like those described here are reversible, but retooling of parenting strategies or even serious damage control is required to get the child back on track. Some basic parental guidelines, strategies, and explanations follow; note that these may also apply to other parent-child problems (besides media-related ones) as discussed in chapters 1, 2, and 3.

Get at the root of the child's behavior!

Why does the child escape into excessive exposure to media?

Little Eileen's energies and talents had simply not been directed toward other worthwhile tasks or activities. In her world, the media were permitted to rule! Preston's behavior reflected social isolation at school. Withdrawn and too shy to make friends, he was looking for some form of meaningful interaction that could engage his energies and compensate for his loneliness. Celeste's quest for thrills and a romantic attachment, reinforced by her naiveté and lack of experience, made her a prime target of predators who prey on the confusion and vulnerability of teenagers. Hers was a case of curiosity and innocence gone wrong.

In each case, the child was sending out messages and signals. These warning signs needed accurate interpretation if the parents were to get at the root of the problem.

Plan strategies to redirect the child's behavior!

Once the root of the problem is identified, what changes in parenting strategies may be needed to correct the behavior?

Mom Sandra needed to plan and restructure Eileen's daily schedule in cooperation with the babysitter. Other feasible, alternative activities—playing with toys, outdoor play, visits to a park, reading, simple chores, coloring, "play dates" with other children—needed consideration in combination with a reasonable amount of viewing of selected television programs and videos (a suggested maximum of two hours per day). *Sandra also had to train the babysitter* in the new routine and help her appreciate the benefits to the child. On weekends, Sandra herself would have to sustain a modified schedule to keep the momentum going and avoid backsliding into bad media habits. Initially, the restructuring would require adjustments by everyone. Until the tantrums subsided and Eileen found joy in her work of play and simple chores, steady monitoring and follow-through were essential.

Preston's parents needed to unite in devising a plan to draw their son away from his growing addiction to computer game play. *Together with Preston*, they had to develop a balanced routine to redirect his attention and energies to study, chores, hobbies, and sports. This plan would include the continued playing of computer games—but of well-selected games, at designated times, and of specified duration. Consistent follow-up and implementation of the plan would be required for its success. Meeting with Preston's teachers would help bring to light further insights into his temperament and socialization skills. Perhaps the teachers could identify a friendly classmate whom Preston could invite over for play. If possible, father and son could go on outings, engage in sports, or play computer games together.

Upon noticing Celeste's preoccupation and troubled manner, her parents needed to take prudent steps to learn the underlying cause. Commonsense intuitions about the emotional state of a girl in the early teenage years would have helped. They could have inquired tactfully among her siblings and friends.

Once it was clear what was going on, they needed to explain to Celeste the threat of cyberspace predators, help her change her e-mail address immediately, monitor her use of the computer, suggest better uses of her leisure, and consult her teachers about her academic performance and behavior in school. *Sensitive to the adolescent's hormonal and emotional changes, caregivers need to nip problems in the bud through vigilance, caution, and intervention, rather than engaging in denial, alarm, and panic.*

Communicate parental strategies clearly, concisely, and firmly but with caring and concern!

How do caregivers convey changes in childrearing once these are decided upon?

Initially, Sandra *needed to communicate with her babysitter* the rationale behind the new schedule of activities, generate enthusiasm for the changes, and demonstrate any new skills that would be required of the babysitter and Eileen. She also needed to explain the new activities to her daughter in very simple terms. In most cases, a very young child responds positively when presented with meaningful, structured tasks of play and chores responding to the child's inner longing for learning, doing, and order.

Sandra and the babysitter might offer Eileen some simple choices involving favorite books or toys. *To monitor the situation, Sandra could make random telephone calls from work to spot-check with the babysitter and Eileen (while also listening for the noise of the television). Perhaps she could ask a neighbor or relative to look in occasionally until the schedule was in place and being observed. Consistency of strategies and follow-through are crucial.*

Preston's parents needed to communicate with each other about their son's development and parenting strategies in raising a very shy child. Fundamental elements of a sound strategy include: open, caring, patient communication with the child; continuing encouragement without aggressive pushiness; family activities that foster socialization with friends, neighbors, and relatives; and extra responsibilities at home or in the classroom to promote interaction and build the child's self-confidence.

Celeste's parents needed to keep communication lines open by avoiding accusations and judgments, and not letting the situation deteriorate into a power confrontation. It was their job to express their genuine concern, firmly and with affection, and elicit their daughter's ideas about solutions to the situation and alternative leisure activities. They could ask her to help plan family activities or one-on-one encounters, such as mother-daughter or father-daughter lunch dates. Celeste should be encouraged to invite friends over so that, among other things, her parents could get to know them.

Reexamine the exercise of parental authority!

How does the caregiver routinely discipline the child and help the child internalize self-control?

Is this done in an *authoritarian* style that tends to provoke timidity or rebellion in the child, or a *permissive* style that sets no boundaries and limits, spoils and pampers the child, and fosters self-centeredness and self-righteousness? Through an *ambivalent* style that vacillates between authoritarianism and permissiveness, confuses the child, and may lead to his manipulation of the parent? Or is the style a more effective, *democratic* one that respects the child's dignity, sets parameters and limits, dialogues and gives explanations, and follows through with appropriate, meaningful punishments that teach the consequences of unacceptable behavior?

In all three cases described above, the parents apparently had opted for a form of permissive indulgence that failed to set boundaries and parameters helpful to the child in developing inner emotional control. Giving in or failing to set limits does not foster maturity. It leaves the child to flounder, experiment, escape, test limits, and rebel, or else to take control of the parent-child relationship. Parents have the right to control, exercise influence, and discipline the child, but they must appreciate that the correct goal of controlling, influencing, and disciplining is the *internalization of self-discipline* in the child! All disciplinary measures or control techniques must therefore be directed to the end of self-discipline—a foundational good habit of work.

As a working mother, Sandra had slipped into media indulgence without discerning its possible bad effects. Preston's parents likewise tended toward permissiveness and tolerated his excessive computer play. Celeste's parents failed to set any limit on her computer use and exercised no precautions about cyberspace predators. Only when these parents observed "acting out" or social isolation or a change in demeanor on the part of their child did they react.

Spend time with the child and express LOVE!

How much time does the caregiver spend with the child and how is love expressed?

Whether parental time with the child is restricted or plentiful, every child deserves the love and respect of a caregiver who expresses it in everyday life. Although psychologists encourage "quality time" with the child in the absence of "quantity time," nothing is more effective than meaningful bonding and attachment in developing honesty, trust, and security in

79

the relationship ... and this takes time! Love can be expressed through *attention, affection, approval, acceptance,* and *appreciation.*

Expressions of Parental Love

When the parent shows . . .

- **Attention,** the child feels *valuable.*
- **Affection,** the child feels *lovable.*
- **Approval,** the child feels *capable.*
- **Acceptance,** the child feels *respectable.*
- **Appreciation,** the child feels *responsible.*

Through healthy bonding and attachment with caregivers, the child develops obedience, healthy self-esteem and self-respect, respect for others, confidence, and trust. These are the traits that form a valuable, likable, capable, respectable, and responsible worker.

Seek professional guidance when appropriate and as needed!

When is it advisable to seek professional help?

In all three cases above, the parents—with revised and retooled parenting practices, effective communication, and continual follow-up—could help redirect the child away from excessive media usage toward the meaningful work of play, study, chores, and activities. On the other hand, all three cases could require professional help if the parents are in denial and fail to respond to the child's trouble signals.

If parents feel helpless and incapable of dealing with a problem or they make no attempts to gain control of a situation, or if the child is unresponsive to all efforts to help, counseling is advisable. Other serious underlying factors may be involving in the child's escape into media—the death of a loved one, marital breakup, move to another city, exclusion by peers, or something else.

Favorable Resolution of Cases

All three of the cases described here resolved favorably! Parental concern, determination to follow through, and the child's willing participation were the key factors.

Eileen found joy in her new activities. Her tantrums eased because of the challenges and satisfaction that came from her work of play and chores.

In time, with parental guidance and love, Preston was able to detach himself from excessive computer game play. Meanwhile, he had made friends with a classmate, an avid skateboarding enthusiast, who encouraged him to take it up. Preston's parents learned to appreciate the needs of their shy son and were happy that his attention was redirected toward schoolwork and a new activity—even though they now worried that he might get hurt!

At first, Celeste could hardly imagine that her chat room friend wasn't the cute seventeen-year-old basketball player of her dreams. But the lewd photos alarmed her enough to open up to her parents. Fortunately, she had not divulged her full name, address, school, or telephone number to the predator. She changed her e-mail address immediately and resolved to avoid chats, except with known friends.

Her parents networked with other caregivers to alert them to the menace of cyberspace predators. They made them aware of the easy access predators have through chat rooms and Web sites that allow children to post "blogs" or personal data, including photos of themselves and their friends.

Cyberspace offers unprecedented possibilities for a knowledge explosion that can be harnessed for enormous good. It has the potential of developing global citizens. But it may also threaten cultural identification and good values. Information overload, distraction, unsupervised exposure to harmful programs, and child exploitation are among the dangers. Parents need to be alert.

In essence, media management calls for *knowledge, understanding, gate-keeping; control, involvement, vigilance,* and *role modeling by caregivers*—all should aim at empowering the child to make effective use of media as tools for doing the real work: *play, study, chores, hobbies,* and *activities.*

Rapid changes in technology ensure quick obsolescence. Today's "in" gadgets may soon be outdated. What are considered short-term positive effects of media may actually morph into negative long-term impacts.

Parents can anticipate some likely outcomes of prolonged media usage but must turn to the results of scientific research for further clues. Periodic updating on media effects is a vital part of media management. This requires reading books and parenting magazines, attending seminars, workshops, and parent-teacher meetings, exchanging experiences and insights with other parents, being involved in advocacy campaigns and lobbying.

For Reflection

1. *"Parents could once easily mold their young children's upbringing by speaking and reading to children only about those things that they wished their*

Cont'd.

---

children to be exposed to, but today's parents must battle with thousands of competing images and ideas over which they have little direct control." (J. Meyrowitz) Any thoughts to add?

2. Have you traced your child's "media history" on a weekly basis—number of viewing hours, kinds of programs watched and computer games played, behavior after heavy exposure or night-time viewing (e.g., nightmares, aggression), perceived positive and negative effects on behavior?

3. What would happen if multimedia use were excluded from family life for two weeks as an experiment? How do you think each member of the family would be affected? What readjustments would have to be made in family relationships?

4. What good values is the child internalizing from media that inspire him in his work? What negative values?

Postscript

FOUR RECOGNIZABLE SYMPTOMS:

The Disease of Work

The Disease

"Work is a disease that we should be eager to catch! It has four recognizable symptoms." No, this is not one of Papa's gems of wisdom, although he would have loved it. I heard it many years ago, date and source forgotten. I remember thinking at the time, "How clever! I will pass this on to others."

With full apologies to whoever originated the thought, I want to use it to help synthesize the contents of the book and leave you with a lingering illness you cannot shake!

The dictionary tells us that a disease is a harmful development, a condition that impairs the performance of a vital function. But the "good disease" of work is anything but harmful. It keeps idleness at bay and promotes the attainment of such vital goals as earning, learning, competence, mastery, self-actualization, teamwork, service, and goodness.

Symptoms

A symptom is defined as subjective evidence of a disturbance, something that indicates the presence of disorder. Indeed, the symptoms of the "good disease" of work are indicators of disturbances, for work provokes development and change and prompts improvement. The diagnosis is based on the symptomatology of work as a *chronic, progressive, contagious,* and *incurable* "good disease."

- **Chronic** because work is an activity that fills and structures human life. Marked by long duration, it begins in the early years through tasks that engage the child in learning and doing, e.g., play, study, chores, hobbies, activities, parttime jobs, and care for the environment. The child gravitates toward work naturally and feels a void or frustration if his capabilities do not receive meaningful challenges to his attention, energies, and commitment. In the process, work evolves into a dependable, persistent means to develop talents and virtues. Always present, the child slowly personalizes its meaning, purpose, and value, but he needs training, guidance, and encouragement to appreciate the *what, why,* and *how* of work.

- **Progressive** because as competence at work increases, so do positive attitudes, efficiency, productivity, and self-confidence. Through gradual improvement and mastery of skills, the child develops good habits or virtues related to work: industry, diligence, responsibility, cooperation, perseverance, courage, fortitude, self-discipline, and self-respect. In time, the child slowly develops the mindset and qualities of a professional who seeks the highest standards of excellence in work. Along the route, media may have beneficial or adverse effects, largely dependent on the caregiver's media management and controls, on the child's attitudes and practices in work.

- **Contagious** because the caregiver's good work is an example that inspires imitation. The child is motivated to emulate the role model. When the caregiver sets realistic expectations for the child and provides opportunities for doing good work, the child internalizes standards and practices. As he cooperates and develops team spirit, he strengthens himself as a responsible citizen who participates and provides service to the common good. The cycle of contagion is renewed each time the child sets a good example to his siblings or cousins, friends, classmates, and teammates. *When good work is passed on from one generation to the next, history repeats itself and a legacy is in the making.* The positive ripple effects contribute to family, community, and nation building and redound to world peace and prosperity.

- **Incurable** because work is an unwavering lifetime illness with no foreseeable remedy in sight! Once it has become a habit, good work provides opportunities for livelihood, self-expression, socialization, and character building. As the child matures into adulthood and struggles to uphold ethical standards, he enhances his dignity and self-respect and emerges as a beacon of integrity to others. In the process, he slowly comes to the realization that *the good disease of work links past, present, and future generations . . . with one another and with eternity!*

Any thoughts to add?

In Review

INTEGRATION CHARTS

In Review synthesizes the essential concepts related to the meaning, purpose, and value of work. For the benefit of readers who teach child development or family psychology and education, or who conduct seminars on the work of children, the following integration charts may be of help.

The charts for chapters 1, 2, and 3 synthesize the essential *understanding, attitudes, skills, and habits that parents and caregivers are called upon to develop in the child.* Each chart should be viewed from top to bottom and across chapters to see the successive nature of development: from early childhood when foundations are laid; to middle childhood when the range of work expands; to adolescence when expectations are higher, capabilities have matured, and a fuller scope of work can be appreciated. Understanding, attitudes, skills, and habits assumed to have been developed at an earlier stage are not repeated in the chart at the next stage. If they have not been internalized at the appropriate stage, they need to be fostered during the next one; the earlier the internalization, the easier it will be to avoid resistance and negative dispositions. For chapter 2, a circle chart, organized according to the *four dimensions of work: economic, personal, social, and ethical,* presents an integrated overview of the purposes of work. The chart for chapter 4 summarizes the *caregiver's understanding, attitudes, skills, and habits necessary for the exercise of effective media management.*

IN REVIEW: Chapter 1 Recreation: *The Meaning of Work*				
Caregiver of child in . . .	**Understanding**	**Attitudes**	**Skills**	**Habits**
Early Childhood (0–6 yrs.)	Function of work: a task and an activity Achievement of work: through play and simple chores	Appreciation of work as a natural activity	Following instructions of a task, activity, toy Care of books, toys, materials, furniture	Understanding of importance of work Understanding of instructions Joy in play and chores Order in work
Middle Childhood (7–12 yrs.)	Function of work: a duty and process Achievement of work: through study, chores, play, hobbies, activities, e.g., sports	Appreciation of work as a means to an end and source of satisfaction	Logical, orderly plan for work	Understanding of goals, techniques, consequences of work Concentration and focus
Caregiver of Adolescence (13–19 yrs.)	Function of work: a challenge and opportunity; a lifelong undertaking Achievement of work: as in middle childhood; a part-time Job	Appreciation of work as a reality of life	Follow through to completion of work Follow-up evaluation	Understanding of short- and long-term effects of work Commitment Perseverance Diligence Responsibility Humility

CHAPTER 2: The Purpose of Work

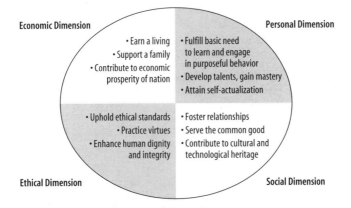

Economic Dimension

Personal Dimension

- Earn a living
- Support a family
- Contribute to economic prosperity of nation

- Fulfill basic need to learn and engage in purposeful behavior
- Develop talents, gain mastery
- Attain self-actualization

- Uphold ethical standards
- Practice virtues
- Enhance human dignity and integrity

- Foster relationships
- Serve the common good
- Contribute to cultural and technological heritage

Ethical Dimension

Social Dimension

IN REVIEW: Chapter 2
The Pie Factory: *The Purpose of Work*

Caregiver of child in . . .	Understanding	Attitudes	Skills	Habits
Early Childhood (0–6 yrs.)	Purpose of work: fulfillment of a basic need to learn and do something well	Openness to learning and socialization	Coordination Dexterity Socialization skills	Understanding the purpose of work Joy in work Order
Middle Childhood (7–12 yrs.)	Purpose of work: development of competence and self-confidence	Sensitivity to work as ongoing, cumulative, and facilitative Sensitivity to work as a link with others	Organization Planning Execution Cooperation	Self-discipline Diligence Responsibility Patience Perseverance Determination
Caregiver of Adolescence (13–19 yrs.)	Purpose of work: enhancement of self-actualization, identity, and independence	Appreciation of work as a source of income and opportunity to develop talents Sensitivity to work as service to the common good and nation	Sound judgment Practical and technical know-how Teamwork Foresight Insight Hindsight	Fortitude Service Generosity Courage Optimism Prudence Accountability

IN REVIEW: Chapter 3 My Gift: *The Value of Work*				
Caregiver of child in . . .	**Understanding**	**Attitudes**	**Skills**	**Habits**
Early Childhood (0–6 yrs.)	Value of work: Discovery of the wonders of nature Care for nature and the environment	Awe of the wonders of nature Personal accountability for nature, material world, and personal possessions Appreciation for caretakers of nature and the environment	Know-how in caring for nature, material things, and personal possessions Good manners	Gratitude and respect for nature Obedience to caregivers Respect for others Appreciation and kindness Order Patience
Middle Childhood (7–12 yrs.)	•Value of work: Usage, or improvement of nature and environment Mastery of skills Service to others	Opportunity for improvement Development of citizenship and spirit of service and sharing	Competence Proficiency Participation in groups Coordination with others	Self-discipline Industry Responsibility Cooperation Honesty Fortitude Service Generosity Cheerfulness
Caregiver of Adolescence (13–19 yrs.)	Value of work: Enhancement of dignity and integrity Respect for dignity of others	Respect for ethical standards Responsible use of freedom Professionalism	Sound judgment Practical and technical know-how Foresight Insight Hindsight	Self-respect Empathy Prudence Conviction Persistence Courage Resilience Commitment Optimism

IN REVIEW: Chapter 4 Kidnapped: *Media at Work* Media Management Guidelines for Parents and Caregivers				
Caregiver of child in . . .	**Understanding**	**Attitudes**	**Skills**	**Habits**
Early Childhood (0–6 yrs.)	Function of media: a channel for entertainment, information, and education Exercise of parental authority Criteria for media selection and evaluation Effects on child development	Appreciation of media as an invited family guest Appreciation of developmental tasks and needs of the young child Interest to keep abreast of research on media effects	Screening and selection of relevant and age appropriate programs Controls for duration of media usage, location, days Planning, scheduling, implementation Monitoring Follow-up	Respect for rights of child to good programming Responsibility to child Prudence in selection of programs Consistency in enforcing rules ROLE MODELING of caring and concern
Middle Childhood (7–12 yrs.)	Importance of media controls Need for explanations and dialogue with child Multimedia joint participation and co-viewing Alternative activities to media usage, e.g., sports, hobbies, reading	Confidence in parental authority Sensitivity to changes in child behavior Appreciation of importance of media and its management Sensitivity to messages and signals projected through media, e.g., violence Openness to networking with parents	Critical thinking and discernment of programs, games, advertisements Consistency in parental control techniques Follow-through of controls Creative strategies to maximize usage and control, e.g., parent-activated blocking options on browsers, software packages	Understanding of effects of media exposure Vigilance Accountability Communication ROLE MODELING of self-control
Caregiver of Adolescence (13–19 yrs.)	Child's sensitivity and vulnerability to values projected through media, e.g., on violence and sexual behavior	Need for vigilance Sensitivity to e.g., changes in child's behavior, social networking via Internet	Networking techniques Strategies to get feedback	Vigilance Responsibility Defense of / and respect for dignity of child

Cont'd.

Caregiver of child in . . .	Understanding	Attitudes	Skills	Habits
Caregiver of Adolescence (13–19 yrs.)	Parental networking and advocacy	Openness to parental linkages and campaigns against cyberspace crimes	Organization and participation in campaigns, lobby groups that promote e.g., child's rights, consumer rights, anti-pornography advocacy Selection of counseling services, as appropriate and needed	ROLE MODELING of temperance, fortitude, caring

Notes

Chapter 1

1. M. Montessori, *The Absorbent Mind* (Oxford: Clio Press, 1988); M. Montessori, *The Montessori Method* (New York: Schocken Books, 1964); E. Hainstock, *Teaching Montessori in the Home* (New York: New American Library, 1968).

2 John Paul II, *Laborem Exercens,* On Human Work (Vatican:Vatican Polygot Press, 1981), 16.

Chapter 2

1. P. Fagan, "The Right of the Child to the Married Love of His Parents." Keynote The International Federation for Family Development (IFFD) 16th International Family Congress, New York, October 2004.

2. M. Montessori, *The Absorbent Mind*, 155.

3. J. Escriva, *Forge* (New Rochelle: Scepter, 1988), 245.

Chapter 3

1. F. Sheen, *God Love You* (New York: Image Books, 1981), 16.

2. D. Yankelovich, "New Rules in American Life: Searching for Self-fulfillment in a World Turned Upside-down," *Psychology Today 15*, no. 4 (1981): 35–91, in M. Csikszentmihalyi, *Finding Flow* (New York: Basic Books, 1997), 49.

3. H. Gardner, M. Csikszentmihalyi, and W. Damon, *Good Work* (New York: Basic Books, 2001), 15.

4. M. Csikszentmihalyi, *The Evolving Self* (New York: Harper Perennial, 1993), 33.

5. M. Csikszentmihalyi, *Flow* (New York: Harper Perennial, 1990).

6. C. Peterson and M. Seligman, *Character Strengths and Virtues: A Handbook and Classification* (New York: Oxford University Press, 2004).

7. P. Vitz, "Psychology in Recovery," *First Things 151* (2005): 17–22.

8. H. Keller, *http://www.quotationsbook.com/authors/3972/Helen_Keller*

Chapter 4

1. American Academy of Pediatrics Media Education, *Pediatrics 104*, no. 2 (1999): 341–343.

2. N. Zill, "Does Sesame Street Enhance School Readiness? Evidence from a National Survey of Children," in S. Fisch and R. Truglio (eds.), *"G" is for Growing: Thirty Years of Research on Children and Sesame Street* (Mahwah, NJ: Lawrence Erlbaum Associates, 2001), 115–130.

3. J. Wright, et al., "The Early Window Project: Sesame Street Prepares Children for School," in S. Fisch and R. Truglio (eds.), *"G" is for Growing*, 97–114.

4. A. Huston, et al., "Sesame Street Viewers as Adolescents: The Recontact Study," (2001), in S. Fisch and R. Truglio (eds.), *"G" is for Growing,* 131–144.

5. D. Anderson, et al., "Researching Blue's Clues: Viewing Behavior and Impact," *Media, Psychology 2*: 179–194, in S. Fisch, "Children's Learning from Television," *Televizion* 18/2005: 12.

6. K. Hymowitz, "On Sesame Street, It's All Show," *City Journal* (Autumn 1995). *http://www.city-journal.org/html/5_4_on_sesame_street.html*

7. D. Christakis, et al., "Early Television Exposure and Subsequent Attentional Problems in Children," *Pediatrics 113,* no. 4 (April 2004): 708–713.

8. National Television Violence Study, "Facts about Media Violence and Effects on the American Family," *Media Scope*, February 1996. *http://www.babybag.com/articles/amaviol.html*

9. N. Minow, "Are 'Educational' Baby Videos a Scam? Research Lacking to Support Claim," Special to the *Tribune,* December 14, 2005. *http://www.commercialexploitation.com/news/babyvideosscam.html*

10. APA Online: Psychology Matters, "Undoing Dyslexia via Video Games." *http://www.psychologymatters.org/dyslexia.html*

11. L. Shapiro, *How to Raise a Child with a High EQ* (New York: Harper Collins, 1997), 309–311.

12. V. Strasburger and B. Wilson, *Children, Adolescents, and the Media* (Thousand Oaks, CA: Sage Publications, 2002), 123, 125, 130, 131, 134.

13. APA Online Press Releases. "Childhood Exposure to Media Violence Predicts Young Adult Aggressive Behavior, According to a New 15-Year Study" (2003). *http://www.apa.org/releases/media_violence.html*

14. T. Robinson, "Reducing Children's Television Viewing to Prevent Obesity," *Journal of the American Medical Association 282* (1999): 1561–67. *http://www.jr2.ox.ac.uk/bandolier/booth/hliving/ObTV.html*

15. Donnerstein and S. Smith, "Sex in the Media," in D. Singer and J. Singer (eds.), *Handbook of Children and the Media* (Thousand Oaks, CA: Sage, 2001), 289–307.

16. N. Postman, *The Disappearance of Childhood* (New York: Vintage, 1994), 137.

Index

A

activities. *See* work
addictions, 59
  computer games and, 76
  media usage and, 67
  sexual, 72, 73
ADHD. *See* attention deficit
  hyperactivity disorder
Adolescence (13-19)
  chores and, 17, 38
  media usage and, 15, 17,
    70–73
  money, use of and, 40–41
  Opportune Moments, xvi, 16–18,
    40–42, 57, 58–59
  peer pressure and, 30
  role modeling and, 16, 18, 42
  socialization and, 59
  study and, 38
  television and, 70–71
  virtues and, 39, 42, 54–55, 59
  work, attitudes toward and,
    20, 38
  work, meaning of and, 15–18
  work, purpose of and, 38–42
  work, value of and, 54–59
advertisements, 29, 68
allowances, 17, 31, 36–37

American Academy of Pediatrics,
  63
American dream, 28
Animal Planet, 48
attention deficit hyperactivity
  disorder (ADHD), 65
attitudes
  Adolescence (13-19) and, 20
  caregivers and, 21
  consumerism and, xv
  formation of, xiv, 18–21
  parenting and, 20–21
  work, meaning of and, 18–21
  work, value of and, 48
authority, parental, 78–79

B

Baby Einstein, 66
Baby Mozart, 66
Back on Track
  communication of parental
    strategies and, 77–78
  expression of love and, 79–80
  media usage and, 73–75
  parental authority and, 78–79
  redirecting behavior and, 75–77
  spending time with children
    and, 79–80

Early Childhood (0-6 years)
  and, 35, 50
fostering, xiv
media exposure and, xvi
Middle Childhood (7-12) and,
  36, 38
parenting and, xv
practice of, 32
work, meaning of and, 21–22
work, value of and, 48, 50
volunteering, xv, 56

W

Walt Disney Company, 66
work
  attitudes toward, xv, xvi, 18–21,
    38
  benefits of, 18
  consumerism and, xvii
  dignity of, xiii, xvi
  dimensions of, xv, 27, 30,
    31–32, 33–35, 40–42
  disease of, 84–86
  family and, xiii
  functions of, xv, xvi, 2

importance of, xiii, 18
joy of, xvii, 18, 22, 54
mastery and, 2
meaning of, xv, 1–23, 88
media usage and, xv, xv–xvi,
  61–73, 91–92
order and, 5
play as, xv, 4–7, 9–10
purpose of, xv, 24–43, 89
as recreation, 1–3
satisfaction of, xvii, 2, 12, 15,
  18, 47
service and, 39, 45–46
study as, xv
team-, xiii, 19
universal phenomenon of, xiv,
  23, 40
value of, xv, xvii, 44–60, 90
volunteer, xv, 56
Work Attitudes Seminars, 27, 39
workers, dignity of, xv, 39, 43, 48,
  49, 60
The Work of Children (Esteban),
  xvi–xvii